WHEN MACHINES TEACH

Designing Computer Courseware

ARNOLD KELLER
Concordia University

1817

HARPER & ROW, PUBLISHERS, New York
Cambridge, Philadelphia, San Francisco, Washington,
London, Mexico City, São Paulo, Singapore, Sydney

Sponsoring Editor: Alan McClare
Project Editor: David Nickol
Cover Design: James Angelus
Text Art: Fineline Illustrations, Inc.
Production: Willie Lane
Compositor: Donnelley/Rocappi
Printer and Binder: The Maple/Vail Book Manufacturing Group

WHEN MACHINES TEACH: Designing Computer Courseware

Library of Congress Cataloging-in-Publication Data

Keller, Arnold.
   When machines teach.

   Includes index.
   1. Computer-assisted instruction—Authorship.
2. Instructional systems—Design.   I. Title.
LB1028.6.K45   1986   371.3'9445   86–29575
ISBN 0-06-043591-7

86 87 88 89 9 8 7 6 5 4 3 2 1

4/27/87   B+T   22.50

Contents

Preface

This is a book about the design of courseware—that is, the teaching materials with which students interact when they're taught by computers. It is both for people who are interested in producing their own courseware and for people (such as evaluators) who are interested in learning about basic design principles. Readers need not be computer experts to write the kind of courseware that appears in the first part of the book. They should, however, be familiar with at least the basics of programming. Later chapters describe work that does require more sophisticated programming skills, and if readers lack them, they should be prepared to work as part of courseware production teams.

The grand (and seldom achieved) goal of courseware is to give the student a worthy substitute for a human tutor. This is done not to replace teachers but to free them to do the things no machine can. When we free the teacher from mechanical or time-consuming activities, we hope to extend our resources to give more students the individualized care that produces excellence.

Courseware is different from either hardware (the machines themselves) or software (the programming instructions to run the machines). Courseware consists of everything that goes into the creation of a tutorial lesson delivered on a computer, from deciding what is to be taught to determining the best way of presenting it. Regardless of the subject matter or level, there are principles and techniques common to all courseware. And while this book draws largely upon school and college examples, the fundamental ideas are the same for trainers in government or industry.

A unit of courseware attempts to teach a significant part of the syllabus without a teacher's direct intervention. This distinguishes it from other kinds of computer education having to do with programming, computer literacy, or using the computer as an adjunct or support to some other activity. Courseware (as we use the term here) is always about a specific subject like math or biology or English. The courseware designer's job is to specify and produce materials that solve the instructional problem of how to bring together one of those subjects with a particular learner.

This book proposes a systematic process for courseware design. The usual temptation when writing programs is to sit at a terminal and bang away until something runs. That's more than just inefficient; it also loses sight of the whole integrated relationship of student, subject matter, goal, and machine. So we need a set of replicable procedures to ensure that nothing is overlooked. This isn't to suggest that we replace the inspiration and spontaneity of the brilliant designer with mechanical plodding. But we need a rational approach that makes it simpler to account for each thing that goes on and to pinpoint each thing that goes astray.

Most of today's courseware needs major rethinking. Too much of what we have available is "scripted" and quite like its immediate ancestor, programmed instruction. The difference between them is that one is delivered by a machine and the other by a book. Both programmed instruction and scripted courseware share the same behavioral roots with a learning theory that prescribes a certain approach to teaching: Take a big chunk of instruction; break it into smaller chunks; present these chunks to students so that they can respond in smaller chunks yet. Typically, the student enters no more than a single letter or word. This sort of programmed reponse simply doesn't go far enough to reflect anything very complex. More importantly, it makes little use of what the computer can do that other media cannot.

Having said that, we are going to spend some time looking at how to construct scripted lessons, because they make good introductions to the basic techniques of courseware writing and employ techniques that can be elaborated beyond the simple multiple-choice frame. Scripted courseware also provides practical programming exercises for someone getting started. And finally, scripted courseware can be of value to students when the objectives are simple and straightforward. But there are definite limits, and we have to make them clear from the outset. The issue is one of "appropriate technology," when and where to use something: which brings us to another major assumption operating here.

Frequently, we shouldn't use computers at all. We can, of course, write courseware that presents screen after screen of text, freeing the student from the supposedly onerous task of turning pages. But why should we? There is no reason not just to assign a book when the situation calls for it. Books are certainly more portable, at least as cheap, easier on the eyes, and more convenient. The same basic caveat holds true for other media as well. Knowing when *not* to use computers is as important as knowing when to use them, and we should keep that distinction sharp. Otherwise, we build Rube Goldberg contraptions that, however clever they are, are the wrong means in the service of the right goals.

It's also useful to say what this book isn't. It's not about hardware. I will assume that the machine you use is more than a home-style device primarily intended for games. What we'll be writing won't require massive amounts of computer firepower, although some of the programs described were written first on mainframes. Today's micros, however, are fast overtaking the speed and memory of the giant machines of just a few years ago.

Nor is this book about programming languages. There are lots of texts available about BASIC or LOGO or APL and the many other high-level languages. Throughout, I will assume that you either can now or very soon will write simple programs. Nor will I discuss, except in passing, "authoring languages," the special packages designed for writing courseware. They have their uses and their limits too, as we'll see. For the programming examples, we'll use "pseudocode," that is, English-language directions that say what to do but that couldn't run on any machine.

Neither is this book about instructional design *per se,* although I do treat it in the context of designing courseware. There are many excellent books devoted to that subject exclusively, and my intention is not to repeat what readers may find there. It goes without saying that courseware, like other kinds of teaching, has to be founded on sound principles of instructional design. My interest here is how those principles operate when we teach with a computer.

And this book is most assuredly not about whether computers are good or bad, if they can think, or if we all will become soulless robots in the vast and blinking arcade of life. These moral and philosophical questions, while real enough, are irrelevant here. I'm assuming that you have decided to use computers to teach with and have made up your own mind about the ethics involved.

Finally, some words about organization. This book grew out of a course in computer-assisted instruction for teachers who had received training in basic programming. That course took them from writing relatively simple, scripted branching lessons to more complex courseware. The organization here reflects such instruction, and the book is in two parts: Part One (Chapters 1–6) shows how to write scripted and generative courseware; Part Two (Chapters 7–11) is more descriptive than prescriptive, dealing with principles of advanced courseware design, rather than pseudocode for specific lessons. Here is a breakdown of what chapters are about what topics:

- Chapter 1 gives an overview of instructional design, presenting both a theoretical model of a courseware environment and a practical model intended for designers involved in courseware production.
- Chapter 2 leads the reader through the actual steps of writing scripted, frame-based lessons.
- Chapter 3 does the same thing for generative courseware.
- Chapter 4 deals with graphics, discussing both why they are important and how we can incorporate them into our designs.
- Chapter 5, about "calcraft," is a compendium of techniques to fine tune lessons and make them easier for students to use.
- Chapter 6 addresses the issue of getting started and deciding whether there is evidence that courseware is the best solution to the educational problem we're trying to solve.
- Chapter 7 (the first chapter in Part Two) discusses the reasons why we have to go beyond scripted courseware.
- Chapter 8 looks at the design principles of educational simulations, one alternative to scripted courseware.
- Chapter 9, the first of three chapters about "intelligent courseware" (another alternative), discusses master performer algorithms and heuristics that provide courseware with the intelligence lacking in scripted lessons.

- Chapter 10 looks at ways of modeling the student that go well beyond the simple recording of right and wrong answers.
- Chapter 11 examines a number of tutoring strategies that make explicit the proper times for a lesson to intervene in a student-courseware dialogue.

Several of the chapters include exercises that you are invited to work at.

A few words on terminology. Throughout, I use CAL to refer to computer-assisted learning, rather than the somewhat more common CAI (for computer-assisted instruction). CAL is a broader term that includes tutorials, games, simulations, and intelligent programs. CAI, on the other hand, generally has meant only scripted, multiple-choice lessons.

Let me conclude with some gloom and doom. Most courseware, commercially written or otherwise, isn't very good. There are exceptions, of course, but they remain exceptions. People often confuse the value of programming computers with what they turn out. Or else they seem to assume that just because something is on a computer, it's intrinsically better. It isn't, although that may be hard to admit after spending many hours writing a lesson that doesn't teach much of anything. Writing good CAL doesn't come easily, and despite glowing predictions of a fabulous future, there are no guarantees that the computer won't become just something else that teachers once plugged into the wall. Certainly, when it comes to courseware, there will be no quick fix. That said, there's still much that can be done and much more to find out about, and I hope this text helps you towards that.

ACKNOWLEDGMENTS

A number of people were good enough to read this book in its early drafts, and I would like to thank them here: James Laffey, San Francisco State University; Allen Mandell, Old Dominion University; Jaime Palavicini, Concordia University; Marilyn D. Ward, Western Illinois University. At Harper & Row, Allen Dykler first encouraged me to write this book and my editor, John Willig, patiently guided its development. David Nickol and his staff made the manuscript better than it was. At Concordia University, my colleagues and students waited through a number of false starts for my ideas to take shape. To all, my thanks. And for the deepest help of all, to Polly Horvath and Jonathan Keller, my gratitude and love.

                                                                                    Arnold Keller

one

THE BASICS
OF COURSEWARE
DESIGN

chapter *1*

Instructional Design for Courseware

IN THIS CHAPTER

■ We will be introduced to two *instructional models* for planning courseware:
    1. a theoretical model of the components of a courseware environment
    2. a practical model specifically for the courseware designer
■ Each model helps us to recognize and say what we want to do and, used together, makes instructional decisions more accurate.

TALES FROM THE CRYPT

Here's an old joke: A general is being shown the newest, costliest, and supposedly most sophisticated computer for training military planners. "Will there be war or peace?" he asks. Lights flash, motors whirr, beepers beep—and the computer eventually displays a single word: "YES."

"YES WHAT?" the general roars.

"YES, SIR!!!" the machine roars back.

Here's another story, albeit from the early days of CAL: My seven-year-old son was having trouble memorizing multiplication tables. I thought it would be "educational" and "wholesome" and "fun" for him to sit at my office terminal and try a math drill that someone had put on the time-sharing system. Feeling pretty smug at my enlightenment and pretty sure about the magic of technology, I came back about a half hour later and found him in tears. "It won't let me go away," he cried. Every time he'd finish a problem, the machine would give him a new one. "How much is 9 × 7?" it would insist. "How much is 12 × 9?" "How much is 5 × 8?" My son just wanted to draw pictures on the stationery for a while. Whoever wrote the thing had assumed that students would just wander off when they had had enough. But my son knew a key rule for being a good kid: Do What I Tell You.

Generals can take care of themselves but kids can't. There's not much funny when teaching doesn't know what it's talking about, or worse, who it's talking to. Put yourself into some honest-to-IBM, real-life courseware: You enter a right answer with two decimal places but the lesson tells you you're wrong because it can calculate only to one decimal place. You hit RETURN instead of the space bar and the screen fills with "ERROR 97." You try a question a few times, reach the point where you don't know what the right answer is, aren't likely to figure it out, and just want to go home. "No, that's *still* not it," the lesson cheerfully admonishes (and mentions something about your tenth miss). You find it hard to be a true believer in the computer revolution.

Such bugs are, no doubt, fairly easy to fix. But here are some other, less readily fixable ones: A geography lesson gets its geographical facts wrong, saying that Canada's Northwest Territories are a province. A biology program hums merrily on (with lots of "Happy Face" drawings), oblivious to the yawning student hitting keys at random. An electronic grammar workbook dutifully collects all the Choice As, Bs, and Cs, and announces "You had 58.7% correct" without even the vaguest attempt to say what that might mean about how well you write. No doubt all these lessons began with a store of good will; good will is not enough.

Even joining good will to hard work sometimes produces only Topsy-like lessons—they just grow without much purpose. This doesn't mean courseware designers should forget about sudden bursts of insight. But what they usually need most are a few rational procedures, given CAL's penchant for making Murphy's Law sound rather cheerful.

PLAN OR BE PLANNED FOR

We can, goes the warning, either plan or be planned for, but with courseware, the consequences of not planning are particularly serious. The absence of a good design plan doesn't lead to a lesson being controlled by alien forces but to it not being controlled by anything at all—except perhaps random events. The happy, serendipitous moment that can mean so much in a classroom can't happen in a computer lesson, if by happy we mean instruction that successfully directs the student's attention and introspection through some particular topic. So while classroom teachers or tutors have the luxury of thinking on their feet to take advantage of the unplanned, courseware designers must specify what will happen under what conditions. And for that they need an instructional design.

INSTRUCTIONAL DESIGN: THE SYSTEMIC AND THE SYSTEMATIC

Instructional design is the planning of learning, and, as such, gives both practical and theoretical help for thinking systematically about educational systems. At a practical level, an instructional design scheme leads us through a thorough consideration of the things that constitute a learning event, from what the student already knows about a subject to the arrangement of chairs in the room. However, even the best plan can't be an algorithm or recipe that step-by-step guarantees perfect learning. It is instead a heuristic, a collection of general principles and proven practices that lead us—albeit often fuzzily—toward what is essential.

At a theoretical level, an instructional design scheme makes explicit the systemic nature of learning, which is not reducible to a given student, teacher, or topic, but involves all three, with myriad variations of competing and harmonizing relationships. It is at the student's peril that we neglect any. Human students, human teachers, and subjects of human concern are all systems of great complexity that become yet more complicated through their coming together with one another. We need a plan, therefore, to approach all this complexity before we can hope to shape it into a context for learning successfully.

COMPUTERS ARE FAST: ARE THEY SMART TOO?

Before we look at such a plan, we should ask a few questions about computers, not about their hardware but about their potential as teachers. Everyone knows that computers are fast, but for courseware speed means little in itself. In the first place, speed cannot provide an "intelligence" that goes beyond the intelligence programmed into it. A lesson delivered via the computer cannot be intrinsically smarter than its programmer.

The relative smartness of computers is much in dispute among researchers in artificial intelligence (AI), some of whom claim that computers do learn and so can move past what their creators know. Certain programs can add new experience to their store of facts, for example, and thereby change their future behavior. But as critics of AI have argued (although not speaking directly about courseware), the only real intelligence in programs that learn lies in the original instructions that tell the machine when and how to modify itself, and those instructions remain resolutely human.[1] Certainly, that a computer performs a task does not necessarily mean it's intelligent enough to teach it.

Regardless of who's right, the practical task of writing courseware makes us focus on the role of human designers, not simply because they instruct the computer how to solve some problem but, more crucially,

[1] For the computers-can-learn side, see Winston 1984; for the other, see Weizenbaum 1976 or Schank 1984. For a splendidly balanced and clear account, see Boden 1977.

because they also must instruct the computer how to teach the solution. And so far, no computer has learned to do that by itself. In short, we can't argue that a computer lesson is inherently smarter than its designer, only inherently faster.

INTERACTION: THE MAJOR ELEMENT OF COURSEWARE

But with speed comes the chance to interact. Although each exchange between learner and instructor remains a product of the human mind, we can now have lots of these exchanges. And a difference in number makes for a difference in kind. Consequently, what the computer permits that other media (except the human teacher) don't is interaction. Whatever question we display is displayed virtually instantly. Whatever response we make to the student usually can be made almost as fast—assuming we know how to respond. All this may be obvious; a lot of courseware ignores it nonetheless.

MAKING USE OF SPEED: SHOOTING ALIENS IN A BARREL

Let's consider what speed makes possible. Suppose you wished to write a very uncomplicated game where players must (yet again) save the world from the evil Klingons who are hiding behind camouflage. To do that, you might have players manipulate a joystick so that a cross hairs on the screen is positioned over a possible location of an incoming spaceship. If ship and cross hairs are at the same place when a player hits the fire button, the program blows up the ship; if not, the game sends out a message like "You were too much to the right and too high." Let's ignore for now whatever else such a game should have. Figure 1.1 shows one primitive way of giving simple instructions to the computer, which in turn will show players how to correct their aim.

The program must first determine the locations of the ship and of the cross hairs when the player hits the fire button; if they coincide, the program redraws the ship as blowing up. If the shot has been off the mark, the program calculates the distance between the cross hairs and the ship and sends out a message. Each time players fire, they set in motion the actions of the program. In the space of a few seconds, a lot of information can be sent back and forth, all in the service of ridding the world of Klingons.

Most people would object (and rightly so) that nothing much is being learned here, and no one would put forward the arcade as educational model—entirely. But the game does provide a clear example of what a computer does best: respond to a response. The effect of an arcade game is engaging because a player is the focus of attention at every moment; every move is the most important thing going on. Combine this with sound, bright lights, and competition, and you have the arcade industry. The challenge for a courseware designer is to take this same power of interaction and get it to do something more than explode spaceships.

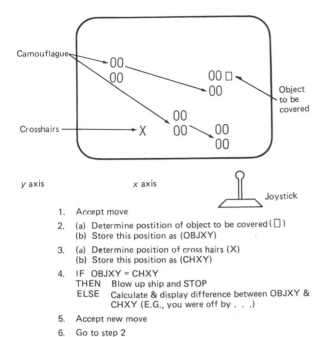

1. Accept move
2. (a) Determine postition of object to be covered (□)
    (b) Store this position as (OBJXY)
3. (a) Determine position of cross hairs (X)
    (b) Store this position as (CHXY)
4. IF OBJXY = CHXY
    THEN   Blow up ship and STOP
    ELSE   Calculate & display difference between OBJXY &
            CHXY (E.G., you were off by . . .)
5. Accept new move
6. Go to step 2

Figure 1.1 A Continuous Monitor for a Simple Arcade Game

INTERACTIVE TUTORIAL LESSONS

Courseware could be a highly interactive medium, then, if it exploits the computer's speed. But what kind of activities accomplish that? A few possibilities are branching, data storage and retrieval, and graphics.

Branching Computer tutorials can branch quickly, jumping to new places in a lesson and bringing new material to the display far faster than a student could turn pages of a book. Of course, if what's brought in is only what could be found in any workbook ("The answer was choice B"), the speed is wasted since the difference between waiting a microsecond and a full second (or even two or three) for such skimpy help isn't likely to matter. But if the material consists of explanations or examples or practice problems, all keyed directly to what the student needs, then rapid branching creates a powerfully different medium.

Data storage and retrieval Computers can store, find, and modify information at great speeds. As machines have evolved in the last few years, the amount of such information has grown tremendously and will again. Courseware designers can write programs, for example, that let students access large data bases; the information can then help put students in a mode of decision making rather than one of learning facts for their own sake. The speed with which we can look up things and see the relationships can make a great difference. A simulation about the population growth, for example, might be more powerful if it provided immediate answers about how many people live in a city or how many people had moved somewhere else. That inexpensive microcomputers now routinely have huge memories is more than a vaguely interesting technical note. It means that large amounts of information can be programmed, and this in turn allows the teaching of complex subjects.

Graphics   Most people are usually delighted with their first exposure to a good computer graphics program. That's because computer graphics need not be fixed forever like pictures in a book or even fixed the way motion pictures lock images into a single sequence. Instead, people can issue commands and the computer will change its display.[2] Rather than a static, one-way transmission of pictures, a computer graphic can change when we want it to. Again, it is really a matter of using the computer's speed to do the dog work—redrawing the screen as learning requires.

The ability to bring in new material, to give access to data, to make images respond—all done with great speed—are three major abilities of the computer that CAL designers can exploit.

IMAGINING INTERACTION: COURSEWARE AS ENVIRONMENT

We can think of courseware generally as an environment through which students move and change what is displayed as they themselves are changed; that is, as they learn. This is quite different from one-way media such as books, slide-tape, or television. It is different even from the classroom where it is unlikely (though possible) that the teacher can adapt to the needs of every student every time. At its very best, a courseware environment approaches the powers of a tutor, someone concentrating all attention on a single learner, adjusting the teaching to each response. What exactly might such a tutor do?

WHAT GOES INTO AND WHAT GOES ON IN THE COURSEWARE ENVIRONMENT

What follows is a model of the courseware environment. Not much of what is available today adheres to this model, but several programs (described in Chapter 11) do have most of these features. The model, therefore, doesn't purport to describe most current courseware; it does, however, outline the theoretical underpinnings for what should be there. We will assume for now that the necessary thinking has been done to make us reasonably sure we

---

[2] Although we're speaking now of images as they're displayed on a computer screen, the images could also be on videodisc and videotape, access to which the computer could control.

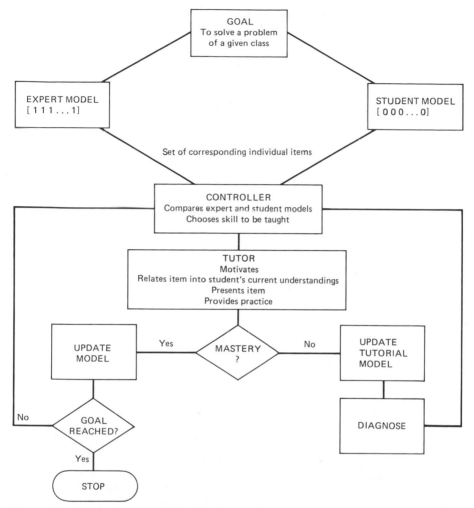

Figure 1.2 The Courseware Environment

want to use a computer.[3] Figure 1.2 illustrates a model of the courseware environment. The model has seven basic components:

1. A *goal* for the lesson, expressed as a typical problem the student must solve.
2. A *master-performer representation,* showing each action an expert takes to solve the problem and reach the goal.
3. A *student model,* corresponding to the representation of the expert, with exactly the same number of elements. The model is updated after each exchange.

[3] Chapter 6 will go into this issue fully.

4. A *controller,* which manages the flow of instruction in the following ways:
   a. by comparing the current state of the student's abilities with the expert's
   b. by choosing an appropriate item to be taught
5. A *tutor,* which carries out the actual teaching (including offering practice sessions), according to a predetermined tutoring strategy.
6. A *tester,* which decides if an item has been mastered.
7. A *diagnostician,* which attempts to determine where and why the student may have difficulties.

THE GOAL: SETTING A TYPICAL PROBLEM

The first component of the model is a goal expressed as a problem we want the student to solve. Here are a few examples of goals expressed as problems:

How to:

> recognize the nominative case
> set the correct aperture on a camera
> write a running computer program
> reconcile a bank statement
> change Fahrenheit into Centigrade
> do mixed calculations
> parse a sentence
> solve a linear equation

A goal is not a behavioral objective; it is less specific about the details of the task, the conditions under which the task must be done, and the precise degree of mastery needed. Unlike the specification of a behavioral objective, a goal requires us to set a typical problem for the master to work on, one that is sufficiently representative of its class and not merely a single, isolated example. If a representative problem isn't found, a solution may not be a general one. That would, of course, weaken the assumption that we can legitimately infer mastery of an entire topic from a student's ability to solve the goal problem.

A goal must also be broken down into either a set of actions or components of knowledge (with each element in the set an "item"). In this way, a goal statement when decomposed depicts unambiguously what an expert would do or have to know if faced with the problem the student is trying to solve. Here are some *caveats* about defining goals.

Goals must be observable   A goal may be only a broadly defined summary of what an expert knows or can do, but it must be observable. We have to be able to see someone doing it or have them describe their actions. If we can't see someone doing a task, we can't describe it to the computer. "Writing clearly" or "adding well" are not observable; "punctuating with less than one mistake per page" and "adding without error" are.

Goals have to be worthwhile Not everything that can be taught should be taught. Quite often in industry, for example, managers often find problems that don't require new training but better supervision or new equipment. There's no reason to teach keypunching, for instance, when data is entered at terminals. Similarly, a master geographer may know all about finding coordinates on a map, but teaching the economic effects of lakes and rivers on nearby cities needs only a very cursory discussion of map reading. A goal may also be too easy to be worthwhile: few office workers need formal training with most telephone equipment.

Goals have to be attainable That a goal is worthwhile does not mean it's attainable. Teaching someone to take an adequately lit picture is possible with a computer that can simulate the effects of adjusting aperture and shutter speed. But teaching someone to take an "aesthetically satisfying" picture asks far more of teacher time and student talent than we can normally expect. Similarly, teaching someone the dates and places of major battles requires little more than flashcards; teaching them the underlying causes of war requires far more.

MASTER-PERFORMER AND STUDENT MODELS: KNOWING WHAT, HOW, AND WHO

From the Goal to the Master-Performer Solution

Once a typical problem has been found that can stand as a worthwhile and attainable goal, its solution must be expressed as the set of skills or knowledge an expert has but a student lacks. To make this transition, we must either have a thorough knowledge of what we want to teach or have access to an expert who does. Where there is no clear path to a solution, we can sometimes settle for the rules of thumb which experts use. For the moment, let's assume we know what an expert would do first, second, and so on, given our typical problem.

Mapping a Master's Knowledge

Figure 1.2 shows that the goal must be represented or mapped as the specific steps taken or items of knowledge possessed by a master (or indeed several such masters, if we will permit alternate solutions). Such a map can take the form of either a network of related ideas or an algorithm that specifies procedures an expert takes to solve a problem.

From Master Performer to Student

We need a master-performer model not only to solve a problem but to show where a student might deviate from an expert. The student, in effect, is an apprentice whose skills are an incomplete subset of an expert's.[4] The initial representation of students shows that they have only some of the master's knowledge, with their unlearned concepts and skills marked on the model as needing attention. The student model expresses where students turn left instead of right, say yes instead of no, or where their actions and the expert's actions don't match in other ways. The chapter on student models develops this idea.

Student models are critical. With them, we can then go beyond what is most often meant by "individualization," that is, merely letting students set the rate at which they proceed, as in a programmed text. To speak, therefore, of "twenty third-graders" or "apprentice electricians" isn't good enough. We want to say why this student makes this response so that we can decide to offer *this* instruction next. Like a human tutor, courseware needs to know (or at least make educated guesses about) the specifics of what the student knows or doesn't.

The Notation for the Master-Performer and Student Models

In Figure 1.2, the master's set of skills are shown as a series of 1s. This means it is TRUE (in the logical sense) that each necessary skill or piece of knowledge exists. The student's map is a corresponding set of 1s and 0s for each element in the master's model; a 1 means that it is true that the student knows that item and 0 means that he doesn't. At the start of the lesson, the controller sets all elements to 0; the results of a subsequent pretest indicate where 1s can be put. As the student goes through the lesson, the controller updates the model and 1s replace 0s. When no 0s are left in the student model, the current goal has been achieved.

CHOOSING WHAT TO TEACH: THE CONTROLLER

A controller decides what needs to be taught by registering which items have been marked as not learned and selecting one accordingly. The controller takes into account what students know at any point and what they must know to continue. It can act in concert with students, permitting them to select any of a number of topics which they have a reasonable chance of mastering. For example, a student may wish to learn Topic A; the controller decides if that is a reasonable choice in light of what the student currently knows. The degree of cooperation between the two is a matter of instructional strategy. The key notion for now is that some means must exist to pick a topic that is both missing in the student's repertoire and attainable, given what the system knows about the student.

[4] Not every CAL researcher accepts this notion; it does limit the user to learning only what the program can do and no more. (See Goldstein 1979 for a discussion on this point.) The brilliantly intuitive student who can see beyond the teacher is not given all he might be. In practical terms, however, the argument is less convincing since the same objections could be made about any brilliant student and any average teacher. A fair description of what teachers do, after all, is narrow the gap between their own abilities and their students'.

Moreover—and this is central—the controller works not just once at the beginning of the session but continually. Each sample of student work provides more information and that in turn permits a better decision about what next to present. After each exchange, the controller updates the model and uses the new information in its next instructional decision.

TEACHING WHAT IS TO BE TAUGHT

After the controller selects a topic, the tutor must "teach with practice." The term is deliberately vague since several choices may exist to teach the same material. A good tutoring strategy will have alternative ways of presenting the same material, not only for different students but for different efforts by the same student. That is, if one method of presentation hasn't worked for a particular student, the tutor must note which one it was and choose another the next time. We'll examine some examples of rules for tutoring strategies in Chapter 11. Among the possible actions are to

- motivate
- fit the current item in the student's existing intellectual framework
- present concepts and rule
- provide practice

For instance, suppose we are teaching about carburetors in internal combustion engines to a high school class. We first must show that carburetors are important. After that, we could present a written explanation with some drawings; a programmed, "page-turning" text with multiple choice questions; or an animated presentation. This instruction should be incremental, starting with concepts we can assume the student knows and then introducing new ones. We could, however, also simulate various carburetor settings, letting the student see the effects of changing the amounts of fuel and air admitted into the combustion chamber.

Generally, we match our goals and objectives to a particular CAL mode. Here is a list of possible activities and a match-up between various possible modes of CAL and objectives:

Modes	Used for
Flash card	Rote memorization
Drill and Practice	Reinforce skill already learned
Tutorial	Teach new material
Game	Learn/practice a skill
Simulation	Explore a previously learned model

TESTING FOR MASTERY

Our next step is to test what the student has learned. Here we can follow Gordon Pask's (1975) suggestion and require students to demonstrate their grasp of the material in some novel way, rather than having them simply repeat what they've been told. Pask speaks of a "teachback" mode. In some cases, this asks students to manipulate a model of the skill being taught in a way a master would. Where this is not possible, they must at least answer a question that hasn't already been expressly answered. We prefer that students show they know *how*; when that's impossible, we settle for them showing they know *that*. The designer's starting point in testing, therefore, must be "What kind of activity would allow me to infer that this person knows what has been taught?"

CHOOSING ANOTHER TOPIC

When the student masters an item, it's marked as learned on the student model. If the student hasn't mastered an item, the program acts as a diagnostician and tries to determine why. Chapter 10 will deal with this difficult question. For the moment, however, let's make the assumption (although it is a large one) that we have found the student's trouble. As we place new information in the student model, the controller has richer information to choose new instruction. The whole process of choosing, teaching, testing, and diagnosing continues until there are no more unlearned items and the student has met the initial goal.

At that point, the controller acts as a higher-level traffic manager, directing the student into other lessons depending on what's needed and what's available. Moreover, in a system in which several alternate lessons exist to teach the same skill, the controller can match students to the style of learning they prefer or is the most beneficial.[5]

NEW TECHNOLOGY, OLD PROBLEMS

Courseware does not make old problems fade away; indeed, they can become more acute. Some such examples are intervention, motivation, control of learning, and participation.

Intervention   Most courseware has to be interactive yet operate without human intervention. When things break down, no one will be there to set them right. It is, of course, possible to design a lesson that depends on

[5] To use another notion of Gordon Pask, "holist" learners (those who like to get an overview of materials and then plunge in almost anywhere) can be given a map of the subject and permission to start where they choose. Others, who prefer a more structured, "serial" approach, can be taken through the material in a predetermined, fixed order. Any other learning style theoretically can be accommodated, assuming we can articulate what we mean by a particular learning style.

the student being able to call on a teacher. But that requires a very specific design choice. There is no absolute reason why we can't use the teacher or books or anything else with courseware as long as we remember that its use no longer will be self-contained. Unless we can be sure that other things will be there, we should design courseware with the assumption that only the machine and student will interact.

Motivation   Nor can we assume that there will be anyone to intervene when the student's attention begins to fade. Ironically, the power to motivate has been put forward as one of the principal virtues of the computer. Much courseware apparently assumes that the very phenomenon of sitting at a computer induces students to want to learn when they otherwise wouldn't. This may have been true when computers were rarely ever available as learning tools; it is surely less true today. Any teaching can be deadly dull, and delivering it on a computer only means that the dullness gets there faster. Superficial attempts to compete with arcade-type games miss the point: Dazzling graphics or sound effects quickly pall if they aren't in the service of something more substantial than just getting a user's attention.

Motivation must come from the traditional source: a recognition by users that what they're doing is important to them. Without a sense that the student's own interests are being talked to, all the dazzling light shows will not count for much.[6] Indeed, motivation, rather than coming from the machine, probably still comes best from the very human teacher who explains why the student needs the CAL lessons in the first place.

Who controls learning?   Much research has gone on about whether authors or students should decide what's taught and when. Again there are no hard and fast answers. Assuming that all parts of a CAL lesson have been written, and assuming also that we can show that particular students perform better when allowed to control the direction of instruction as well as its pace, there is no reason not to let them. The controller in Figure 1.2 should be a counsellor, keeping students away from topics for which they lack prerequisites. To let students simply choose without such help, however, is to invite their frustration.

Participation   The old saw about hearing and forgetting but doing and remembering is more than just an old saw when it comes to designing courseware. The computer increases participation only when we use it well. Courseware lessons that simply display text like an electronic textbook miss the point of the medium. If lessons only send out information and don't let students interact, why shouldn't teachers simply assign books?

---

[6] This is not to say that courseware shouldn't entertain. Marshall McLuhan once remarked that those who think education has nothing to do with entertainment know nothing about either.

THE SYSTEMATIC DESIGN OF COURSEWARE

A Consensus Model

We turn from a theoretical account of a CAL environment to the operational problems of actually designing courseware. The practice of educational technology over the past twenty years or so has produced a level of agreement very close to a consensus about the process of instructional design. While all designers naturally reserve the right to their own variations, Figure 1.3 shows an instructional design scheme that includes the most common features.[7] In following such a plan, a designer

- begins with a statement of broad goals
- moves on to an analysis of who will be taught
- performs a task analysis
- develops and presents materials
- evaluates the effectiveness of the teaching

Each step is not done once and ignored thereafter; instead, the process is iterative, with many loops back to earlier stages.

Such a model serves well enough in most cases. Certainly, as a rational approach, it is an improvement over *ad hoc* methods where teacher and students never really know what direction a class takes until it's over. But the consensus design does have to be modified for courseware. In the rest of this chapter, we'll get an overview of such a modified plan; later chapters will take up the details.

A Design Model For Courseware

The design process for CAL consists of these steps:

1. see the problem in system terms
2. specify a solution
3. code and make preliminary tests
4. fine tune for easier use
5. do a formative evaluation
6. revise as needed
7. implement
8. perform a summative evaluation and follow-up

Let's examine each in more detail:

1. *See problem in system terms.* We begin by trying to see the whole context of the instructional problem we wish to solve and the evidence that courseware is the best solution. Among the issues we examine are

---

[7] The model in Figure 1.3 is very much in the mainstream of instructional design. The details of many similar models appear in many places; see, for example, Gagne and Briggs 1974; Kemp 1977; Dick and Carey 1978; Romiszowski 1981; Rowntree 1982.

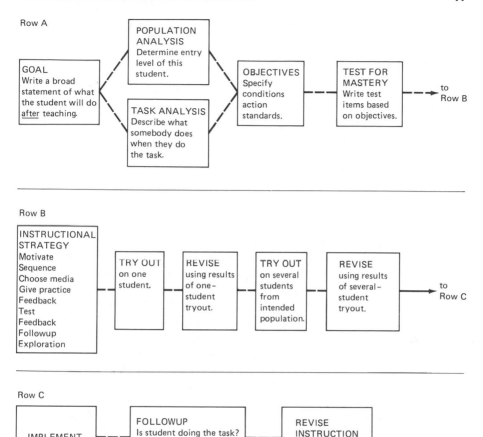

Figure 1.3 The Consensus Instructional Design Model

the boundaries of the courseware or what its scope should be
the discrepancy between the desired and current output
the need for interaction
the amount of complexity we will allow the student to express and
   our ways of coping with it
the possibility of modifying existing courseware

All this comes well before we think of coding or attempting to specify a solution. We first try to see the feasibility of using courseware to solve an instructional problem and then outline a very general and tentative solution. Chapter 6 on the preliminaries of designing courseware goes into this in greater detail.

It's worth reminding ourselves right here, at the outset of design, of a dangerous trap: the solution in search of a problem. This happens when we try to use courseware in places where we shouldn't. Indeed, one potential anomaly of a special instructional design for courseware is that it may automatically presuppose that the computer should be used at all. A good instructional design scheme, quite rightly, leaves the selection of media an open question until at least the basic analyses have been done.

2. *Specify a solution.* Once we've looked at the feasibility of a goal and of using the computer to reach it, we can go on. Still at the planning stage, we begin to fill in details of our proposed solution.

- Locate a typical problem of the kind we wish the student to solve.
- Create a master performer model.
- Define a student model.
- Develop tutoring strategies, a controller, and a diagnostician.

What sometimes becomes apparent as we go beyond general goal statements is that we can't ourselves—nor can any expert to whom we speak—articulate an unambiguous solution to the typical problem we are addressing. But without our gaining a clear sense of a subject, we can't program a computer. In such a case, we have to recognize that we simply have chosen the wrong subject for a computer lesson. Only a human, for instance, can conduct a full Socratic dialogue about philosophy like Socrates—and not too many humans at that. Only a human can make aesthetic and moral judgments with any subtlety. Our medium should not, as we have said, try to be a catch-all solution in search of a problem. It is at this stage we would abort an attempt, before we have committed so much energy that it becomes too painful to give up.

3. *Code and run preliminary tests.* Here we enter code and make sure that it runs, at least sufficiently well for us to continue. Except for the various examples in pseudocode,[8] we won't say very much in the rest of this book about coding. Throughout, we'll assume you can program in some language, or will soon acquire those skills. Even if you are taking a team approach to courseware production, as many designers do, you should at least be able to write pseudocode for the eventual programmer.

4. *Fine tune for easier use.* Here we concern ourselves not with theory but with the craft of CAL. In general, we try to arrange things to make the lesson easier to run: screen design, input handling, and so on. Chapter 5 on "Calcraft" offers specific advice.

5. *Conduct a formative evaluation.* This crucial phase is often ignored— with disastrous results. A formative evaluation identifies a lesson's weak and strong points so that the designer can revise it. Formative evaluation is first done by means of a one-on-one trial where the designer observes a representative student and records what works and what doesn't. Sometimes called *beta testing* (to distinguish it from the *alpha testing* of code in step 3), a formative evaluation can go from several single-user sessions to

---

[8] *Pseudocode* refers to instructions that cannot be run on a real computer but do show the general form the program will take.

trials with small groups. Its importance can't be overstated since it moves the lesson from drawing-board speculations to real-world experience.

Here are some questions a formative evaluation answers:

Do criterion test scores show mastery?
What kinds of errors do users most often make?
Are the errors in the same part of the program?
How much time do users need to complete the lesson?
What instructions (either on how to use the lesson or how to think about its content) are unclear?
Do students have enough places to practice?
Are users motivated by the material?
How accurate is the material?

Here are some ways to answer these questions:

final test results and intermediate scores
error patterns and locations
places where the user asked for clarification
questionnaires
rating scales
anecdotal information
designer's own informal observation and notes
the opinions of other designers and subject matter experts

6. *Revise as needed.* Revision can range from minor tinkering to substantial alteration. The number of times we do formative testing and subsequent revision can't be predicted, of course, except to say "often."

7. *Implement.* This last stage involves the final production, distribution, and use of materials. It can also involve logistical details like scheduling students' time on the computer, arranging for sufficient copies of programs to be available, or setting up equipment. Often, it may mean convincing people to buy the programs and other people to use them.

8. *Perform summative evaluation and follow-up.* We should not forget the necessity of a summative evaluation, which shows us how effective a lesson is at meeting the goals of instructional effectiveness and efficiency. Summative evaluation is done with medium-sized groups (about 30 per group so that we can make legitimate inferences from the results), drawn from the intended population. We use formal experimental designs and subject the findings to statistical analysis, the details of which are available in many books on educational research. The objective, as with the earlier formative evaluation, is to show the designer where to make changes in future versions of the lesson. In that ideal sense, no evaluation is ever really final. But we do reach the point where we have to put the lesson into the real world. Finally, we should do periodic, follow-up testing to see that the system operates as designed.

The design process is not linear but iterative. As we go forward and gather more information, we cycle back to earlier stages to revise and refine.

And this extends beyond the loops we might expect from the formative evaluation. For example, specifying a solution may sharpen our sense of the basic problem. Coding may point out missing elements in our proposed solution. Making a lesson easier for the student to run may lead to major changes in coding.

A CHECKLIST FOR CAL DESIGN

The checklist that follows, like the instructional models on which it is based, is not an algorithm that guarantees a successful lesson. It should be considered a fairly rough, rule-of-thumb guide that increases the likelihood of success by pointing out essential topics and tasks. Here it is:

1. State the instructional problem (if indeed one exists).
   What are the goals of those affected?
   What proof is there that CAL is the medium of choice?
   What are the constraints and resources?
   Is the goal worthwhile?
   Is the goal attainable?
   How feasible is it to attempt a CAL solution?
2. Formulate a brief general statement of intended population—grade levels, assumed skills, etc. How does the proposed lesson fit into their goals and needs?
3. Select a typical problem of the class the student should solve.
   Outline a general solution by representing an expert's repertoire of skills and knowledge.
   Express the formal relationships the lesson will teach.
   Restate them as production rules.[9]
4. Write items to determine current state of student's repertoire vis-à-vis the master's. These may include specific test items or student self-assessment.
   Mark as learned those items the student has mastered before instruction.
5. Articulate a tutoring strategy that sets out the basic sequence of instructional events and provides its rationale. (Draw on previous knowledge, of rules, concepts, skills, and so on.) Consider ways to motivate student.
6. Produce and debug code to
   set and solve problems
   accept and store student's response
   compare student's and computer's solutions
7. Code control mechanism that will direct student either
   to the next topic, or
   out of the lesson (if all topics have been learned).
   Update student model as required.

---

[9] See comments below.

8. Produce and code diagnostic tools. Hypothesize bugs in student's procedure and run problem with bugs inserted. Refer back to both master and student repertoires for specifics.[10]
9. Fine tune the lesson for easier use.
10. Perform formative evaluation with one or more representative students. Check for
    unnoticed programming bugs
    ambiguous instructions
    errors in presentation of subject matter
    places where student attention strays
    speed of lesson
    other lacunae
    anecdotal information
    logistical and implementation problems
11. Revise as needed.
12. Implement.
13. Perform summative evaluation with larger group.
    Produce experimental design to isolate and measure effectiveness and efficiency of program for the intended population.
14. Revise as needed.

Figure 1.4 shows the result of using the checklist to design a lesson about the fulcrum. It is not a running CAL lesson, of course, but only the preliminary notes toward one. There still remains the considerable work of bringing it online and into the classroom. One of the exercises at the end of the chapter asks you to go through it, making whatever improvements you think necessary; our objective here is not to try to produce the definitive fulcrum lesson but to present a way for thinking about such a lesson.

Figure 1.4 Using the CAL Design Checklist

GENERATIVE CAL MODEL

1. GOAL

To understand and manipulate a model of a fulcrum.

2. POPULATION

Junior high school science students, assumed to have multiplication and division skills and to be currently studying various forms of levers.

3. MASTER PERFORMER REPERTOIRE

Can multiply and divide;

Can manipulate fulcrum model so that it balances by changing the distance of either weight nearer or closer to fulcrum or by increasing or decreasing the amount of either weight;

Can substitute numbers into the following formal relationships:

[10] See chapter 10.

    a. $W1 \times D1 = W2 \times D2$
    b. $W1 = (W2 \times D2) / D1$
    c. $D1 = (W2 \times D2) / W1$
    d. $W2 = (D1 \times W1) / D2$
    e. $D2 = (D1 \times W1) / W2$

As production rules:

    a. IF $W1 \times D1 = X$ THEN $W2 \times D2 = X$
    b. IF $W2 \times D2 = X$ THEN $W1 = X \div D1$
    c. IF $W2 \times D2 = X$ THEN $D1 = X \div W1$
    d. IF $W1 \times D1 = X$ THEN $W2 = X \div D2$
    e. IF $W1 \times D1 = X$ THEN $D2 = X \div W2$

4. INITIAL STUDENT REPERTOIRE

Given 2 random numbers

    a. Can he solve Random1 × Random2?
    b. Can he solve Random1 / Random2?

with 100% accuracy.

Given 2 random numbers and their quotient

    c. Can he change values so as to produce a balanced beam? That is, can he solve: If Random1 × Random2 = Result1, what must Result2 be, regardless of the particular values of Random3 and Random4 if the beam is to remain balanced?

with 100% accuracy.

Given 3 appropriately chosen random numbers

    d. Can he substitute numbers into formal relationships (see Master) and solve for the fourth?

with 100% accuracy.

Mark as learned any item for which student has mastery.

5. CHOOSE ITEM FROM MASTER PERFORMER'S REPERTOIRE

Basic Strategy

    a. Be sure student can multiply and divide.
    b. Demonstrate fulcrum via a graphic of a seesaw.
    c. Show how both sides must be equal if a balance is to be maintained.
    d. Demonstrate method of substitution: multiply $W1$ by $D1$ and divide result by $W2$.
    e. Demonstrate with different values.
    f. Let student enter own values either with numbers or by positioning weights on beam.

Rationale for Choosing Topics

IF 4a absent and/or 4b absent, THEN go there.

IF 4c absent, THEN go there.

IF 4d absent, THEN go there.

6. TEACH ITEM WITH PRACTICE

Present concepts as appropriate (balance, equations, substitutions, etc.) and provide examples, practice, feedback. Use graphics showing two weights on either side of fulcrum, changing the mass and location of the weights. Allow student to do same with his object to maintain balance. Simple animation required to show either his success or failure.

7. TEST FOR MASTERY OF ITEM

a. Choose appropriate skill or formal relationship.
b. Generate necessary random values.
c. Solve and store answers.
d. Ask student to manipulate values on the graphic (i.e., ask him to calculate fourth value).

8. MASTERY PRESENT FOR THIS TOPIC?

YES

If original goal reached (i.e., all topics marked as learned), exit from lesson.

If original goal not reached (i.e., not all topics marked as learned), *update* student model to show this topic learned; go to step 5 and choose new item.

NO

Diagnose bug:

a. calculation error: run various "bugs" to see if any result matches student's.
b. Test for idea of balance: can he solve for step 4c?

Reteach topic: return to step 6 and generate new numbers.

9. PERFORM FORMATIVE EVALUATION

10. REVISE AS NEEDED

11. PERFORM SUMMATIVE EVALUATION

12. REVISE AS NEEDED

A few additional remarks might help. Production rules (mentioned in number 3 of the checklist) are IF-THEN statements which, because their logic is so similar to what computers use, are very valuable in representing a subject for a CAL lesson. Chapter 9 covers their form, creation, and use. The references to generating test items (number 7 of the checklist) are only possible for "Generative CAL" which will be discussed in detail in Chapter 3.

SUMMARY

In this chapter, we looked at two instructional design models to be used together to help plan CAL tutorials. The first was a theoretical model of a courseware environment showing its ideal components: goal, master-performer model, student model, controller, tutor, tester, and diagnostician. The second was a practical design model for courseware consisting of the following eight steps:

1. See the problem in system terms.
2. Specify a solution.
3. Code and make preliminary tests.
4. Fine tune for easier use.
5. Perform a formative evaluation.

6. Revise as needed.
7. Implement.
8. Perform a summative evaluation and follow-up.

EXERCISES

1. Restrict the scope of the following topics and write goals for courseware: algebra, modern poetry, chemical formulas, capitals of the world, operating a videotape recorder to view movies.
2. Choose an area which you think is not well taught. Is it a good candidate for courseware? If so, outline a solution based on the two models used here.
3. This chapter listed four problems (intervention, motivation, control of learning, and participation) that become even more acute with courseware. Add and discuss some examples of your own.
4. Revise the fulcrum lesson in Figure 1.4.

REFERENCES

There is something very close to a consensus about what components are necessary for an instructional design model. This is not to imply that all of the authors cited here are in cheerful agreement; however, their similarities are far more important than their differences. The artificial intelligence community is more sharply divided about what constitutes learning. In addition to the works mentioned in the text, Dreyfus's (1972) more skeptical view is worth reading.

Instructional Design

Briggs, L. *Handbook of Procedures for the Design of Instruction* (American Institutes for Research, 1970).
Dick, W. and Carey, L. *The Systematic Design of Instruction* (Glenview, Ill.: Scott, Foresman, 1978).
Gagne, R. M. *The Conditions of Learning* (New York: Holt, Rinehart, and Winston, 1965).
Gagne, R. M. and Briggs, L. *Principles of Instructional Design* (New York: Holt, Rinehart, Winston, 1974).
Kemp, J. *Instructional Design* (Belmont, Calif.: Fearon-Pitman, 1977).
Pask, G. *The Cybernetics of Human Learning and Performance* (London: Hutchinson, 1975).
Romiszowski, A. J. *Designing Instructional Systems* (London: Kogan-Page, 1981).
Rowntree, D. *Educational Technology and Curriculum Development* (London: Harper & Row, 1982).

Artificial Intelligence

Boden, M. *Artificial Intelligence and Natural Man* (New York: Basic Books, 1977).
Dreyfus, H. *What Computers Can't Do* (New York: Harper & Row, 1972).

Goldstein, I. "The genetic graph—a representation for the evolution of procedural knowledge," *International Journal of Man-Machine Studies,* Vol. II, 51–87.
Schank, R., with Childers, P. G. *The Cognitive Computer* (Reading, Mass: Addison-Wesley, 1984).
Winston, P. *Artificial Intelligence* (Reading, Mass: Addison-Wesley, 1984).
Weizenbaum, J. *Computer Power and Human Reason* (San Francisco: Freeman, 1976).

chapter 2

The Design of Scripted Courseware

IN THIS CHAPTER

- We examine courseware in relation to our earlier models of a CAL environment and CAL design.
- We write "scripted," multiple-choice courseware which, although too simple for learning of any great complexity, will introduce us to the basic design of computer tutorials. Later chapters will extend this model of courseware.
- Starting with true/false frames, we then go to multiple-choice and constructed-response frames.
- We extend the model by
    1. linking frames together and branching to different ones, depending on how the student is doing
    2. adding scoring capabilities to each frame
- We briefly examine authoring systems and languages that permit the writing of scripted, multiple-choice lessons.
- In a concluding set of exercises, we go through the various steps for creating simple tutorials.

USING THE CAL ENVIRONMENT TO PRODUCE INTERACTION

Good courseware, like a good teacher, interacts with its students. However, the picture of the courseware environment outlined in Chapter 1 is a static collection of lesson goals, models of master performer and student, and descriptions of controller, tutor, and diagnostician. That by itself only suggests interaction but isn't explicit about how to achieve it. We need to take the elements of a courseware environment and make them interact.

THE USES OF SCRIPTED CAL

The scripted, multiple-choice, courseware we will write in this chapter isn't a model for all computer tutorials but rather a way of getting started using the computer to teach. Scripted courseware is similar to programmed instruction: The lesson presents material in small amounts, asks a question, lets the student respond, says whether the answer was right, and repeats the cycle. We use the term "scripted" because the designer imagines a set of possible exchanges between lesson and student, and writes a script accordingly. Such courseware has limitations but can help students to

> assimilate information
> memorize facts
> learn rules and concepts
> choose among alternatives
> become familiar with problem-solving strategies.

Two fundamental weaknesses of scripted courseware are (1) its weak sense of the material it tries to teach and (2) the limited information it gathers about a student. These greatly constrain the choices a designer can make about what next to present. We should therefore be aware that we're using only a scaled-down version of the CAL environment and its possibilities when we produce scripted courseware.

A SIMPLE MODEL OF INTERACTIVE COURSEWARE

The flow of events of scripted courseware is straightforward:

- The lesson *displays* a message on the computer's screen and prompts the user to enter a response.
- That response is *accepted* and *analyzed.*
- The lesson makes a *decision* about what to display next.

A designer of courseware, then, controls four main processes:

1. displaying information
2. accepting input
3. analyzing input
4. deciding what next to display

Display refers to whatever is visible to the user, be it information about the subject, a question, a command, a picture, or anything else.

Accepting input means that the computer pauses,[1] waits until the user enters a complete answer, and then stores it for future use.

Analyzing input refers to the process by which the computer "understands" what the user means. It can be as simple as matching a single character or as complex as looking for several objects in a densely filled sentence.

Deciding what next to display uses the results of the analysis to select a new display (which may tell students their answers were right, offer another explanation, a new question, etc.); the cycle then repeats itself.

HOW THE CAL ENVIRONMENT BECOMES INTERACTIVE

Courseware interaction results from the designer planning and producing the necessary components of the CAL environment and then setting them in motion. The four-part process of display, acceptance, analysis, and decision describes the results. This differs from describing either the courseware environment itself (what should be there—goal, models, etc.) or the design and production process (what somebody does).

DISPLAY: COMBINING MASTER PERFORMER AND TUTORING STRATEGY

The relationship between environment and interaction can be seen in various ways. For example, a display combines what the master performer knows about a subject with the lesson's tutoring strategy. That is, a decision about what to show the student demands

1. a knowledge of a master performer's skills and
2. a statement when and how to present them

In a simple lesson on world capitals, for example, this may just be the knowledge that Washington, D.C., is the capital of the United States and the directions to say so when the student thinks otherwise. In a more complex lesson, the master performer may know how to parse a sentence; the tutoring strategy would say when each step of the parsing process should be presented, reviewed, practiced by the student, and tested.

ACCEPTING INPUT: KNOWING THE GOAL

Knowing what kind of input to accept first means knowing

1. the problem that the student must solve and
2. what skills or knowledge that requires of the student

---

[1] Pausing doesn't mean that background activities like drawing and redrawing images or keeping track of time necessarily halt; it means that the lesson waits for students to enter their responses as part of the whole interactive process.

In simple cases, we accept just a letter or a word. Elsewhere, we may ask for input such as an algebraic expression, a drawing, or an entire sentence. We can only decide what to accept when we have first planned the environment for a particular lesson and set up a problem that would elicit a good representation of what the student knows.

ANALYZING INPUT: THE STUDENT AND MASTER MODELS

Similarly, analyzing input requires

1. knowing the steps a master performer takes to solve a problem
2. looking for evidence of that in the student's answer

We can't know what to look for in the student's response unless we have first created an expert against whom we measure the student. Again, in some cases (like the courseware in this chapter) analysis might be very simple—we look for a single word or letter. But analysis can be extended to the process of searching in the student's response for several different things combined in several different ways.

DECIDING WHAT NEXT TO DISPLAY: CONTROLLER, DIAGNOSTICIAN MODELS

A decision to display something results from the controller

1. examining an updated student model
2. choosing an item to be taught

Like the display process, the decision requires that a tutoring strategy be in place. We have to choose what to give the student: more practice, a new topic, a complete new start. When the student makes an error, we need a diagnostician to see why. So before we can think about interaction—even as simple as what will be tried in this chapter—we have to plan and then set in place all the components of the CAL environment.

A THEATRICAL METAPHOR OF INTERACTION

The interactive process can be thought of as four actors who respond not only to the user but to each other as well. What the next display will be, for instance, depends on the most recent decision; that decision rests on the most recent analysis, which itself depends on the most recent input the lesson has accepted. Their continuing interactions become progressively richer and more complex as we learn more about the student, but their order—display, accept, analyze, decide—remains invariant. Looked at through this metaphor, the controller plays director, keeping track of each process and coordinating their actions.

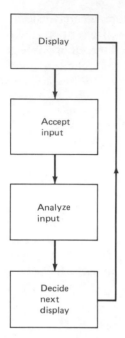

Figure 2.1   The Basic Frame Structure

THE FRAME: A BASIC ORGANIZATIONAL UNIT
OF COURSEWARE

Just as we can group actors into companies, we can group the four processes we're speaking of into frames. It's convenient to think of these four processes as a unit that constitutes a frame: that is, the organizational and structural unit one most frequently encounters in CAL.[2]

Any of the processes or actors can—indeed must—do more. Their roles must be extended and their range of possibilities widened, so that they can cope with the variety of inputs the user is likely to enter. As we go on, we'll see some ways for such elaboration, but we will not be making a fundamental change to the sequence—display, accept, analyze, and decide. Instead, we will be deepening each process. To come back to the theater metaphor, we won't add any new actors but just give them more lines to say.

THE SEQUENCE OF A TRUE/FALSE QUESTION

Courseware built around true/false questions is too primitive to teach very complex subjects, but it will show us the basics of the design process. We'll

---

[2] A frame in this book means the basic unit of display, acceptance, analysis, and decision. The word frame comes from programmed instruction where it designates a chunk of information, frequently with a question at the end, the answer to which the student finds on the next page.

begin by using our four actors to construct the simplest kind of CAL exchange.[3]

The initial display Let's assume that our planning shows a sound reason for asking a True or False question about the capital of the United States. We begin by *displaying* something (a statement to motivate, an introduction to world capitals, a reminder of what's known, etc.). For now, let's display only this:

The capital of the United States is Washington, D.C.: True or False?

(Enter T or F)

Whatever computer language we use will have a command that prints out on the screen what we want to show. Normally, the computer continues executing instructions until none is left. However, we want the computer to stop here, at least just long enough for the interaction to take place and the user to enter T or F.

Accepting input: using variables Our list of instructions to the computer, therefore, must have a line that halts it temporarily. That lets the student enter a T or F, which we have to keep long enough for the analysis of it to take place. If we don't, the answer will be lost to us. We use a variable—that is, a kind of box—to store it.[4] Let's adopt the convention that the student's most recent response always will be in a variable named ANSWER. Many languages let us choose meaningful names for variables so that we can see at a glance what they hold. Where a language permits only letter- or number-variable names (like A or Z9), we can still adopt the convention of reserving the same letter each time for the student answer or score (like A or S).

Analyzing Input Having asked our question, allowed the student to answer, and stored the response in a variable, we analyze the input. In this case, we merely check if what's in ANSWER is exactly T or an F. Given a letter by the student—such as T or F—the computer compares it with what we say is right. The process looks like this:

1. Is what's inside ANSWER the letter T?
2. Is what's inside ANSWER the letter F?
3. Is what's inside ANSWER neither T nor F?

The third condition is a contingency plan; we need to know what to do if a student enters something we weren't expecting.

---

[3] The exercises at the end of the chapter have you begin to write courseware on a computer. For now, you can use pen-and-paper to keep track.

[4] A reminder for new programmers: What varies in a variable is its contents. The name remains the same. We can think of a variable as a post office box with an unchanging number on its outside. Each day things may be placed in there by a clerk and removed by the owner; sometimes it will be empty, sometimes not. Regardless of what's there, the number outside the box never changes.

Making a Decision   We don't have to worry about keeping track of what's true because the computer does that for us automatically. In practice, we combine each analysis with an immediate decision about what to do if something is true:

1. IF what's inside ANSWER is the letter T, THEN display the word "Good."
2. IF what's inside ANSWER is the letter F, THEN display the word "Wrong."
3. IF what's inside ANSWER is neither T nor F, THEN display "Please enter only T or F" and repeat the question.[5]

Figure 2.2 shows some samples of what the screen would look like, depending on what the student enters. Later, we'll see that the analysis (what the IF part says) doesn't always consist of looking for only one item and immediately taking a decision (the THEN part). But for the moment, we can say that if a condition has been met, a particular action must take place. If that condition, however, has not been met, the THEN portion of that line is ignored, and the computer goes to the next line on its list.

And that—in terms of a simple model—is that. There has been

1. a display of material
2. an acceptance of input
3. an analysis of input
4. and a decision to display something else

Taken together, these elements form a frame, a kind of building block for CAL. But it's obvious that nothing has happened that really uses either the machine's power or exercised the student's intelligence. The next step must be to elaborate each element so it can do more, and then to combine and arrange them all to provide richer and more varied exchanges.

EXTENDING THE BASIC FRAME STRUCTURE: BRANCHING

We can extend the basic frame structure in two ways:

1. Make each frame capable of displaying and accepting more than just "True" or "False."
2. Link frames so that a set of them becomes an entire lesson on a single topic.

Taken together, these two strategies produce comprehensive lessons. In theory, we can make any frame respond to any student at any given moment. In practice, that much help exceeds what either a human teacher

---

[5] Programmers will see immediately that this pseudocode is not very efficient; most languages permit these three instructions to be part of a single line. My object throughout is to show the logic of the exchange, not the best way to code it.

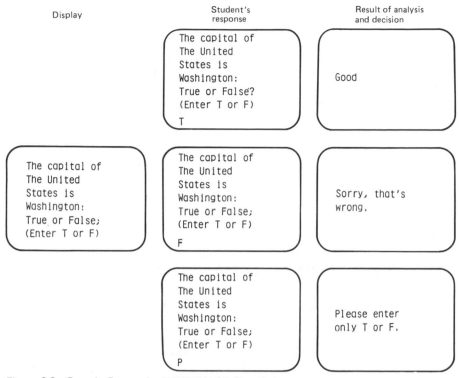

Figure 2.2   Sample Screen for TRUE/FALSE Questions

or a piece of courseware could accomplish. What we can do more readily with courseware is "branch" or jump from one frame to another, and then branch again. The obvious problem lies in writing all the necessary frames, given the limits of our own cleverness and the limits of our hardware. Although the effort may be worthwhile, it's ultimately impossible in the fullest sense. We have to limit our instructional goals, therefore, to what we can accomplish with a restricted number of frames.

DESIGNING BRANCHING PROGRAMS

A branching program takes different students on different paths through the same lesson. Assuming that all students have roughly the same skills, they start at the same place.[6] But the student who answers "A" will go in one direction while the student who answers "B" goes in another. This is because branching lessons reserve one path for a particular idea students may have about the material, an idea that requires a response from the lesson that is quite different from responses to other ideas about the material. The student with Misconception A needs instruction different from the student with Misconception B; they both need something different

_____

[5] Naturally, the results of a pretest can start different students at different places.

from the student with Misconception C (or the student who knows the right answer). However, after the various paths have been completed, all students return to the main stream of instruction, where another part of the subject is taught and where the branching process begins again.

The effect of branching varies from student to student. Someone who gets everything right might go through the frames in a linear fashion: The lesson asks her a question, tells her she's right, and then asks another. A student who meanwhile misses a couple might be sent along a path where he's told he's wrong and given a hint and another try. A student having lots of problems might be sent off to an entirely separate remedial program before being routed back to the main set of frames. Within limits of storage capacity and designer ingenuity, very large lessons can be written. But again, regardless of how large and complex they become, the basic sequence as we have come to understand it holds within each frame: display, accept, analyze, decide.

COMBINING MULTIPLE-CHOICE FRAMES INTO BRANCHING LESSONS

Like True/False Only More So

Let's see how this works in practice by building a branching lesson, using multiple-choice questions. As before, we begin with a *display* that here, naturally, will phrase the question to elicit a single-letter answer (that is, A, B, C, D, or E);

> The capital of the United States is:
> a) Washington, D.C. b) New York c) Los Angeles d) Chicago
> e)Philadelphia

As before, we temporarily halt the flow of the program so that the student can enter an answer; that is, we *accept* input. And again, we'll store it in the ANSWER variable[7].

Multiple Choice Means Extending Analysis

We now extend analysis, looking for more than just one of the two legitimate responses possible in the True/False example. This time, of course, we'll need one IF-THEN for each possibility (A through E). In addition, we'll again include a contingency plan in case we get something other than

---

[7] Another brief note for new programmers: It may appear that since we already have the last answer stored in ANSWER that we'll be letting ourselves in for some confusion, but that's not the case. Whenever we place something in a variable that already exists, the effect is to erase the old value and keep the new one. There's never a time when two values reside in the same variable. That, of course, is no advantage if we wish to preserve the old value. In that case, we should either choose a new name for the second answer, or (much better) copy the old value into a different variable.

letters A or E. For each choice, we provide a different sequence. Figure 2.3 shows how this works.

Frame 1 has five possible paths (A to E) resulting from five possible responses the student can make. Each response leads to a different frame (F1A to FIE in the case of choice A); in turn, each member in this group has five possible choices of its own (for example, F1A can lead to F1AA, F1AB, F1AC, F1AD, or F1AE). The process can continue until the designer runs out of computer memory or ideas about what to put in each new frame. One student, therefore, might go from Frame 1 to F1A to F1AC; a second might go from Frame 1 to FIB to F1BA; and so on. However, when this set of frames has been exhausted, *all* students go to Frame 2, where the same branching process with new frames takes place.

We can express the basic process in highly inefficient pseudocode:

IF ANSWER is A DISPLAY *FRAME A*
IF ANSWER is B DISPLAY *FRAME B*
IF ANSWER is C DISPLAY *FRAME C*
IF ANSWER is D DISPLAY *FRAME D*
IF ANSWER is E DISPLAY *FRAME E*
Otherwise: DISPLAY original question and accept new input.

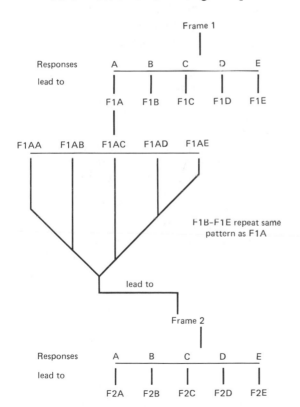

Figure 2.3 Frame-Based CAL: Structure and Possible Paths

The first five lines tell the computer that if some condition has been met, immediately present a new display and ignore the rest of the instructions. Each line has to do its own analysis to see whether its condition has been met. As before, a designer need not be very concerned at first about how the machine actually does this; the designer's most important job is deciding that the condition *needs* to be considered in the first place. That precedes any questions about coding.

Expected Responses: Conditional Branches

As in the True/False example, the computer compares the contents of the variable ANSWER with whatever the designer anticipated might be possible. In the example above, if A is *not* stored in ANSWER, the program doesn't display *FRAME A* but goes on to the next line which checks if the B is stored in ANSWER.

Unexpected Responses: An Unconditional Branch Back

If the computer fails to find any condition true, the final *display* must be shown. The lesson repeats the original question, regardless of what the student has entered. In this example, the designer had a simple-minded contingency plan—repeat the question once more—but there are more helpful things to do, like saying what constitutes "legal" input or noting how many times such a problem has happened.

CONSTRUCTED RESPONSES: ANSWERING WITHOUT PROMPTS

Let's now consider a type of question that retains the logic we're following but requires a different kind of answer by the student. A constructed-response question asks the student to reply without prompting. For instance, rather than display a list of cities, a constructed-response question asks only, "What is the capital of the United States?" Many teachers prefer this kind of question because it reduces guessing.

From the point of view of courseware design, we treat a constructed-response question like a multiple-choice question. That is, instead of looking for single letters, the analyzer looks for whole words. It cannot look for every possible word, of course, but only those we anticipate are most likely to be present in the student's answer. It may seem that we are inviting a far greater range of responses than with a multiple-choice question, but we are not. For just as a lesson can't really say much to the student who enters X instead of A or E, a lesson can't help anyone who thinks &*H2J is the capital of the United States. Looking for a single word is only a bit harder, therefore, than looking for a single letter.

However, more flexible input analysis is possible with constructed-response questions than multiple-choice ones. Here are a few examples of what we can do:

Partial Matches: Accept as correct not only an exact match but one in which the student's answer matches the first, last, and third letters (or other combination) of the answer. For example, *Wishinkton* would be as correct as *Washington*. This forgives typographical errors.

Synonyms: Accept as correct any one of a group of words (for example, Yes, Yeah, Sure, Y, OK).

Key Words: Accept as correct *any* response that contains the right answer (or its alternatives) *anywhere* in it.

Ignore Case: Accept as correct any correct answer, regardless of upper or lower case (for example, car or CAR).

Ignore Punctuation: Accept as correct any correct answer, regardless of punctuation attached to it (for example, car or car!).

Chapter 5 goes into this subject in more detail.

AT THE NEW FRAME

Let's return to the flow of events in scripted courseware. The point of sending someone to a new frame, of course, is that it is best suited to her answer. At Frame A (for the student who said Washington, D.C., was the U.S. capital), the display not only could read something like "Right" or "Very Good" but could be enriched with extra information about the city. At Frame B (say, for the student who chose New York), the display could be, "No, that's the largest city in the United States but not the capital." And so on with specific information for each of the other choices. And as we have seen, we can ask a new question at each frame. Again, in theory at least, the process can continue indefinitely; in practice, computer memories and designer time limit its duration.

RECORD KEEPING FOR SCRIPTED COURSEWARE

Once we have students branching all around the lesson, we need to keep track of where they are and how they're doing. In this section, we'll see how to keep both aggregate and partial scores. Let's start with ways of keeping records about individual frames.

Initializing Variables

We can do record keeping in several ways, and all involve creating more variables. We'll use SCORE to keep track of how many right answers the student has. At the start of the session, we *initialize* SCORE in one of the following ways:

1. Set SCORE to zero: We do this when we want to give points for every correct answer and keep an aggregate score.

2. Set SCORE to N: N can represent how much of a resource is left (seconds remaining, money to spend, number of errors allowed, etc.). We can do this where students compete (against other students or the machine) and their object is to accomplish something before running out of resources.

Incrementing or Decrementing Score

Each time the student branches to the place reserved for right answers, SCORE can be incremented or decremented by a fixed amount. For example, if we are keeping an aggregate score and the student gives a correct answer, the computer takes the current value of SCORE and adds one to it. So, if the student correctly answers the very first question, the new value of SCORE is 0 + 1, or 1; if four questions had already been correctly answered, SCORE would become 4 + 1, or 5. And so on.

Decrementing a score obviously works in the other direction by subtracting some amount. For example, if the computer has a clock, a lesson might deduct the number of seconds elapsed since the last time the student pressed a key or gave a right answer. When SCORE contains zero seconds, the game (or whatever) is over.

Whether incrementing or decrementing, the system need only display a line like this at the end of the session:

"Your score for this lesson is" SCORE

The first part of the line is a simple display like any other; the last part is a command to the computer to display the current value of SCORE.

Recording the Number of Attempts

An important variant of this technique records the number of tries a student has on each question. There are two common uses for this information: keeping an overall score and keeping track of student difficulties.

Keeping an overall score If the lesson gives a different number of points depending on the number of attempts (perhaps three points on the first try, one on the second, zero on the third), then it needs to take the following steps for each question:

1. Initialize a variable called TRIES.
2. Increment it after each try by the student.
3. When the student gets the correct answer, look at TRIES before changing SCORE:
   IF TRIES equals 1, increment SCORE by 3.
   IF TRIES equals 2, increment SCORE by 1.
   IF TRIES is greater than 2, leave SCORE unchanged but display the right answer and go to the next frame.

The last instruction is particularly important because it rescues the student who simply cannot come up with the right answer. Without such a safety net, a question might be repeated indefinitely.

Keeping track of student difficulties   It's helpful to know how many tries students typically take before they get right answers. The student who gets everything right the first time probably needs an accelerated pace; the student who usually takes three tries may need a less demanding lesson. To record this, we could initialize three new variables, TRY1, TRY2, and TRY3. Every time the student answers, the lesson looks at TRIES (set above) before changing TRY1, TRY2, TRY3:

IF TRIES equal 1, increment TRY1 by 1.
IF TRIES equals 2, increment TRY2 by 1.
IF TRIES equals 3, increment TRY3 by 1.

Later, either during or at the end of the lesson, we can examine the three TRY variables to see if a student consistently needs three tries. This might indicate not only something about the student but about the clarity or difficulty of the lesson.

Scores as Vectors: Grouping Answers

There are other ways to keep score. For example, rather than keeping a running count of how many points students have accumulated or how much they have left of a resource, the variable SCORE can be a vector (that is, a kind of list) of 1s for right answers 0s for wrong ones. For example, a list of ten questions might be stored this way:

1 0 0 1 0 0 0 0 1 1

The 1s in positions 1, 4, 9, and 10 show right answers; if the questions are grouped somehow (say, according to different skills we teach), we can locate those positions in the SCORE vector to determine which concepts have been learned. For example, questions 1, 4, 9, and 10 might all have tested multiplication, while everything else tested division. The total score can be found, of course, by adding up the vector.

Vectors for Multiple-Choice Questions

Similarly, we can cluster the distracters on multiple-choice questions to tell us which skills need improving. For example, every wrong answer of a particular type can be always made choice B; each time the student chooses B, therefore, we know a particular mistake has been made and we can increment a special variable accordingly. We would need only to examine the variable periodically to tell if its value were high enough to warrant extra remediation. In practice, however, we wouldn't want to alert test-wise students by always putting the same kind of mistake in the same place. Instead, the computer can record which distracters in which questions show the same errors.

Recording Which Questions Attempted

A variant of using a vector to show skills learned is to create a variable that shows which frames have been visited or which questions tried. This can be used when students decide to quit before completing a lesson. By maintaining records on their permanent file, the lesson can inform them at the start of their next session where to continue without repeating what they've already done.

DECISIONS AT THE END OF A BRANCHING SEQUENCE

Having branched the student to the appropriate frame, displayed some suitable remarks, and recorded the score or type of error, we have to decide where to go next. There are essentially two choices:

1. return all students to a common next question
2. direct each student to a question that his performance calls for

Directing everyone to a common next question is, of course, very straightforward. The program needs only an unconditional branch at every point where the lesson completes remediation or enrichment:

DISPLAY next question

Once there, we repeat the fundamental display, accept, analyze, and decide structure.

THE PROBLEMS OF GIVING INDIVIDUALIZED INSTRUCTIONS

Rather than send everyone through the lesson's major parts in a purely linear fashion—always from A to B to C—we can use the student's record to decide what mode of instruction is best for him: extra help, review and practice, enrichment, or another try. The first option—the linear movement—is the crudest instructionally; but the second, where we branch, can lead to a labyrinth of paths connecting an impossibly large number of frames to be stored and accessed.

In fact, we quickly face an inevitable combinatorial explosion of frames sufficient to the needs of every kind of student. Clearly, we need some middle ground between providing only the same frame for all and trying to ready a frame for every conceivable combination of answers. The problem very much comes from the basic assumptions of the frame paradigm, and we will examine some alternatives to it in later chapters.

PROGRAMMING PROBLEMS WITH BRANCHING CAL

Some programming caveats are in order for branching courseware. The most common way to branch is through GOTO statements available on many languages (even structured ones like LOGO). However, computer scientists generally caution against branching. Indeed, some advocates of structured programming, where each task is broken up into subtasks, try to avoid any branching at all. They argue that excessive use of GOTO commands creates a maze of instructions that becomes very difficult to follow. So many things can change when a lesson runs that tracking its flow or tracing its bugs can become nearly impossible. Moreover, branching can encourage sloppiness in both programming and design style. It becomes all too easy to make things up as one goes along rather than planning each stage. The pragmatic solution when designing scripted courseware is three-fold:

1. Conceptualize the whole program as much as possible before coding it. Such "front-end" planning reduces *ad hoc* solutions.
2. Use subroutines or structured languages. Both can break long lessons into manageable chunks of code, each of which performs a single task.
3. Provide ample documentation, both in listings and in separate manuals, to say what the different lines do.

AUTHORING LANGUAGES AND SYSTEMS

What Some Authoring Languages Can Do

In addition to general-purpose computer languages (such as LOGO or BASIC or FORTRAN), *authoring languages* let designers who can't program produce courseware. Authoring languages typically invoke common sets of actions through a single command. For instance, rather than refer to line numbers, an authoring language may use meaningful names (like Part1).

Similarly, score-keeping functions need not be explicitly seen to by the author; invoking a score feature increments the scores automatically. And so too for such other common courseware actions like stopping the system to accept input, matching the student's answer against what has been stored, and doing management functions. Some authoring languages even help create graphics and provide templates (a kind of blank form) that lead the author through the actual production of the lesson. In short, authoring languages try to free designers from worrying about many routine chores.

What Most Authoring Languages Can't Do

Why, then, should anyone bother learning a programming language if the same results can be accomplished without one? First, results may not be the same. When we buy an authoring language or system, we buy its educational philosophy. While it is indeed true that everything this chapter has so far discussed can be done with a good authoring system, more powerful and flexible design options exist, as we'll see in later chapters.

A few authoring languages (like TUTOR, for instance) sometimes offer these options but many don't. And authoring systems, once in place, are not easily adapted—if at all. For example, intelligent CAL, about which we'll speak in later chapters, needs more than the relatively simple matching-answer strategies that come with most authoring systems. More powerful authoring languages like TUTOR do have some natural-language capabilities and allow for more than simple multiple-choice, but one still is locked into a particular philosophy that limits future choice. Moreover, the more powerful authoring systems themselves require a serious commitment to learn despite the promotional literature that promises easy and painless training. In fact, the time required to master some of these systems is as long as learning many general—and more powerful—programming languages.

In brief, then, whatever the advantages of authoring systems and languages, they have serious deficiencies. If one has no plans to go beyond the branching frame, they will accomplish the necessary tasks. But learning to make that happen might take as long as learning a general language without the compensation of possessing flexibility in regard to machine or courseware philosophy. Authoring languages are best viewed as coding aids; unless they can help design and deliver flexible and complex teaching strategies, they limit, rather than extend, CAL.

SUMMARY

In this chapter, we saw our earlier models of the CAL environment and CAL design did not show the interactive nature of courseware. To see how interaction works, we used a four-part model consisting of display, accepting input, analyzing input, and decision. Beginning with True/False questions, we proceeded to scripted, multiple-choice courseware that, although too simple for very complex learning, introduced us to the basic process of designing tutorial courseware. (Later chapters will extend and elaborate the process for us.) We found we could add to the courseware by (1) linking frames and branching to different ones depending on how students do and by (2) adding scoring capabilities to each question.

Finally, we touched upon the subject of authoring systems and languages. While such systems are capable of producing the simple kinds of lessons, most are neither powerful nor flexible enough to go beyond scripted courseware.

EXERCISES

1. At a computer, display several lines of text to introduce the lesson you are about to write. For instance, you might say something to the student about how to enter answers, what topics the lesson will cover, or how many questions will be asked. Keep your remarks fairly brief.

2. Think up a "True/False" question of your own and display it. Then make the lesson stop long enough to accept the student's answer and store it in a variable. Analyze the contents of the variable, and display either "Right" or "Wrong."

3. Write a new question, extending what you did in Exercise 2 so that the student can choose one of five possible letters. In addition, include a line that presents the question once more if the student's input was not "legal." For each acceptable response, display "Right" or "Wrong" accordingly.

4. Repeat 3, extending it so that the remediation for each of the five choices is different and appropriate. For instance, instead of saying "Wrong," say "No, that's the capital of. . . . "

5. Extend Exercise 4 by routing all students to a second question after they have received remediation. Then write this new question so that it not only will provide a message for each response but will ask a new and different question of its own. These new questions, of course, should be appropriate for the particular answers that made the program branch to them. After these questions have been written (along with their remediation), route all students to a common display. Before you begin to program, sketch a diagram that will show you the various possible paths.

6. Redo any question you've written, changing the multiple-choice format into a constructed response.

7. Keep the score for the set of questions you've just written. Initialize the score variable by setting it to zero. At each line where the student has given the right answer, increment the score variable by one. At the end of the questions, display a line that shows the total score.

8. Keep records to show how many tries students take on each question. Report this to them at the end of the sequence.

9. Personalize your questions by going back to the beginning and adding a display that asks students for their names. Accept the input, store it in a variable, then intersperse it in the subsequent displays so that the computer appears to be addressing students directly.

chapter *3*

The Design
of Generative CAL

IN THIS CHAPTER

■ We explore the possibilities of generative courseware which (unlike scripted courseware) does more than match the student's answer against what the designer programmed into the computer.

  • Generative courseware uses the inherent powers of the computer to build a master performer which itself can create and solve the same problems that we give to student. The great advantage that generative CAL has over scripted courseware is that a very large number of examples can be written using a relatively small number of instructions.

  • Drills are easy to write because the computer repeats its instructions and new problems and their answers are generated.

  • We don't have to limit ourselves solely to mathematics; lessons in the social and natural sciences can also be created, as well as some limited examples in the humanities.

■ We identify two critical requirements for generative CAL:

  1. a way of getting a set of values to work with either from the student, from ourselves, or from generating them randomly
  2. a way of manipulating those values in predictable ways

WHAT GENERATIVE CAL DOES

Generative CAL generates questions and answers. Unlike scripted courseware, generative CAL doesn't require explicit directions for each question or answer. Instead, a single set of instructions creates a very large number of problems to display and solve without the ongoing help of the designer. Generative courseware uses the computer's power to take the first steps towards *intelligent CAL,* that is, courseware that understands what it teaches.

A MASTER PERFORMER WITH NUMBERS

Generative courseware understands its subject in a limited way, of course. It certainly is no HAL, the humanoid computer of science fiction. Historically, computers have most often computed numbers because programmers could describe what they themselves did when they computed. It's easier to list the steps in multiplying two numbers than the steps in knowing what a sentence means. The practical result for courseware is that, in certain subjects, we can build master performers, an essential part of a courseware environment.

A master performer knows something—a series of steps, a set of facts, some rules—and can bring its mastery to bear on a variety of problems. However, the master performer in scripted courseware can't generalize; it knows only what the designer says is right about each and every problem. In fact, it hardly seems true to say a lesson "knows" that Washington, D.C., is the capital city of the United States when it's been programmed to accept only a single letter (T or F or A or B) or even a string of them (W,A,S,H,I,N,G,T,O,N). If the designer doesn't make explicit which letters are right each and every time, the lesson fails.

However, sometimes we can make computers work without explicit and ongoing help. Computer languages allow us to add, subtract, multiply, and divide, and although these abilities have been first programmed by a human, they are sufficiently general enough to work for any set of numbers without much further human intervention. Compare this to a lesson about capital cities: We could write a lesson that knows a lot about Washington, but it still could not generalize what it knows to other cities. However, a computer that adds 22 and 56 can easily add other numbers too. The result is a rudimentary machine intelligence—not human, to be sure—that behaves like a master performer.

WHERE GENERATIVE CAL IS USED

One encounters generative CAL most frequently in mathematical drill-and-practice exercises where students need lots of repetition. (The actual teaching of the skill is done elsewhere, usually in the classroom.) For example, here's a typical exchange:

SCREEN 1

```
Computer: How much is   45
                     +   37
                        ─────
                        [  ]
```

SCREEN 2

The student enters a number, and the cursor moves
to the next column:)

$$
\begin{array}{r}
45 \\
+ \ 37 \\
\hline
[\ ]2
\end{array}
$$

SCREEN 3

(The student enters the last digit and the computer
checks the answer and tells the student the
results.)

$$
\begin{array}{r}
45 \\
+ \ 37 \\
\hline
72
\end{array}
$$

Computer: "No, your answer was too small by 10. You
forgot to carry the 1."

Such exchanges continue for as long as the student needs, presenting
examples in a variety of ways. For example, the lesson doesn't have to wait
until the student enters a complete answer before saying something is
wrong.

Mathematics is the easiest subject to program this way, but not the
only one. In general, any subject is a candidate if we can

1. draw upon a set of values
2. manipulate them in predictable ways

And this—at least theoretically—includes the physical and social sciences
and even the humanities. We'll examine some of those later but start with
a more straightforward example.

THE ENVIRONMENT OF GENERATIVE CAL

Let's suppose students need a subtraction drill. The basic frame paradigm
we've discussed—display, acceptance and analysis of input, and decision—
still holds, but we extend it. To start, we build a *master performer* for the
display that will create and solve the problems that the lesson asks the
student to solve. In addition, we need a *controller* to determine:

1. When to stop giving problems:

   At a predetermined number?

   At a given competency level (like five consecutive right
   answers)?

   At the point when the student wants to stop?

2. When to change the magnitude of the numbers the student subtracts.

3. What help we'll provide for wrong answers.

4. What instructional decisions we will make.

For the moment, let's simply have a variable that keeps track of how many questions have been asked:

Create variable *number.of.questions* and set it to 0

THE MASTER GENERATOR

Since we are going to use the computer's built-in ability to subtract numbers, we don't have to describe subtraction to program a master performer. But we do need numbers for the drill to work with. We get them in two ways:

A prepared list   We can prepare a list of numbers that we want the student to work with (or have the teacher "load" a list at the start of a session). Such a list would generate problems with specific characteristics like steadily increasing numbers or examples that always make the student borrow. With a prepared list, the computer starts at the first pair of numbers and works its way through until the list is empty or the student wants to stop.

Random numbers   Here, the computer generates random numbers and reduces human intervention. We need only tell the lesson the largest number we want produced. The pseudocode to generate subtraction problems looks like this:

Generate a random number up to N and store it in variable *bignumber*
Generate a random number up to N and store it in variable *smallnumber*

N can be any number (up to the limit your system permits) and *bignumber* a variable name you choose.[1] Each time the line executes, the old value in *bignumber* is thrown away and replaced by an entirely new one. Of course, we don't throw away a number without using it but store it instead in a variable. The next line executes the same instructions a second time, changing the variable name to *smallnumber.*

We can make sure that the first number is always bigger than or equal to the second by two methods:

1. Make the current value of *bignumber* the upper limit given to the random number generator when we create *smallnumber.* For exam-

---

[1] Another note for new programmers: If we execute this line with "10" in the place of N, and then display *bignumber,* we might see a 5 the first time, a 3 the next, and a 10 the next after that but nothing larger than a 10.

ple, if *bignumber* presently were 7, the largest possible value for *smallnumber* would also be 7.

2. Check that the second random number is smaller than the first. If it isn't, repeat the instruction to generate the numbers.

DISPLAYING THE PROBLEM

So far, we have two values, and we are ready to display them along with some instructions:

> DISPLAY "HOW MUCH IS:"
>
> > *bignumber*
> > − *smallnumber*

Everything except the variable names themselves is the ordinary kind of display we used in scripted courseware. The lesson displays the message (which can say more than "How much is . . .) and current values of *bignumber* and *smallnumber*. If *bignumber* and *smallnumber* were 25 and 17 respectively, the student would see this:

> HOW MUCH IS:
>
> > 25
> > −17
> > ‾‾‾

One programming note: We must position the numbers on the screen so that they line up in columns.

ACCEPTING THE ANSWER

Once again, we'll use the variable *answer* for the student's response. We have two choices accepting it:

> We can let the student finish entering the whole answer, or
> We can check each digit against what we know is the right one.

Our choice depends on how much we want to intervene. Here's the pseudocode if we take the whole answer:

> Stop executing
> Accept some input
> Store it in *answer*

Accepting input has the same positioning problem as display. We have to accept each digit one at a time, placing it the rightmost empty column; we then shift the cursor one place to the left. In this way, the computer simulates what the student would do with pencil and paper.

THE MASTER SUBTRACTER

At this point, we've generated a problem, displayed it to the student, and accepted an answer. Now we turn to the key difference between scripted and generative courseware. In multiple-choice questions, the lesson compares the student's answer with what the designer said was right. If a designer says New York is the capital of the United States (choice A, perhaps), the lesson can't disagree. But generative courseware doesn't need such explicitness; instead, the computer becomes a calculator and subtracts *smallnumber* from *bignumber,* once more storing the result in a variable we can later access. The pseudocode looks like this:

Subtract *smallnumber* from *bignumber* store result in *rightans*

It is now a straightforward thing to analyze the input and proceed to a decision:

If *answer* is equal to *rightans,* then display "right message"
If *answer* is not equal to *rightans,* then display "help message"

A "right message" can be a word of praise, perhaps followed by a harder problem. A help message can be a simple "Sorry—Think Again" (followed by a loop back to the question) or the lesson's diagnostician can be called and a remediation sequence begun. For now, let's leave complex decisions to the chapter on student models and concentrate on the fundamental structure of generative courseware.

In its barest form, then, here are the steps for designing generative courseware:

1. Display a problem using two numbers (either from a prepared list or random number generator) and ask the student to solve the problem.
2. Accept the student's answer;
3. Analyze the answer by comparing it with what the computer calculated,
4. Decide what to display to the student.

MAKING THE NEXT DECISION

In the final step above, we decide what next to display. Here are some options:

- Increment then examine *number.of.questions* (the variable that keeps track of the number of questions asked). Suppose that we have decided to ask ten and only ten problems; after each problem, we would:
  1. Increment the current value of *number.of.questions* by 1.
  2. IF *number.of.questions* is equal to 10, DISPLAY "Your score is" *score* and stop session.
  3. If not, DISPLAY a new problem.
- Display not only that the answer was right or wrong but by how much the student was off, if appropriate.

    1. Subtract *answer* (what the student entered) from *rightans* (what the computer calculated) and store it in variable *difference*.
    2. DISPLAY "You were off by" *difference*.

- Let students stop at any point. After each question ask "Do you want to stop?" or periodically remind them to enter S whenever they want to stop.
- If errors become too frequent whenever the random number generator produces a number over a certain threshold, lower that threshold. That is, *bignumber* should not be much larger than the biggest number the student appears to handle without difficulty.
- Instead of a running score, keep track of all the wrong answers of a particular kind (for example, failing to borrow); when that variable reaches a given level, route the student to a special remediation section.
- When students reach a specified level of competence (for example, five consecutive right answers), raise the magnitude of the numbers being generated or ask them if they want more practice.

You can add other decisions and let the controller act like a traffic manager to carry them out.

We can, of course, also ask that *bignumber* and *smallnumber* be added together, multiplied, or divided or do some combinations (as in calculating percentage where one divides some number into another and then multiplies by 100.) Our fundamental procedure remains the same:

1. Generate values to use in problems.
2. Have the computer perform the same manipulations on them that we wish the student to do.
3. Compare the computer's answer to the student's.

BEYOND DRILL AND PRACTICE: TEACHING ABOUT FULCRUMS

However useful a math drill can be, it does not exhaust the possibilities of generative courseware. Again, in general terms, as long as we have some place from which to get values and a predictable way of manipulating them, we can design generative courseware. The sciences, using so many formulas, provide a good place to try next.

A Master Balancer

Suppose we want to teach an elementary class a simplified version of how fulcrums work. We can express this idea by way of an equation:[2]

$$W1 \times D1 = W2 \times D2$$

where $W1$ and $W2$ are weights placed on either side of a fulcrum and $D1$ and $D2$ are the respective distances from the fulcrum. This is our master

---

[2] The math here is deliberately simplified to show the structure of the courseware. An object on a seesaw touches it at more than a single point.

performer's expert knowledge. In order to determine if the weights are in balance, the expert multiplies the weight on one side by its distance from the fulcrum and compares the result of doing the same thing with the weight on the other side. The pseudocode looks like this:

1. Multiply W1 by D1 and store the result in variable *side1*.
2. Multiply *W2* by D2 and store the result in variable *side2*.
3. If *side1* = *side2* then display an "It balances" message.
4. If *side1* does not equal *side2*, then display an "It doesn't balance" message.

The messages, of course, can be more elaborate than saying only whether the seesaw is balanced.

Accepting Input

What we haven't decided yet is where those four values (W1, W2, D1, and D2) will come from. We have two choices:

1. Use the random number generator to produce four different values.
2. Ask the student to provide them.

If we choose the first method, we have to be sure that the numbers will be reasonable ones. We can't have W1 at a hundred pounds and W2 a million unless the distances are of the same scale of magnitude. We want not only to get numbers that balance (at least often enough to make the instructional point) but also to have numbers that will produce readily comprehensible results.

The limits on the input we accept must be strongly rooted in what we want to teach, not in computer science. That is, we choose whatever we choose because we know what we wish to accomplish instructionally. If we get all four values from students, we have to decide what will be learned from their just watching the computer display "It balances" or "It doesn't balance."

If, for instance, what we really wish to teach is multiplication, then we might at first forget about fulcrums and concentrate solely on numbers. Later on, we might use the interest in fulcrums to drill the multiplication. If, however, we want to focus on the idea of balance, we should let students choose all values, one at a time, as in a laboratory where they would be given a balance and some weights.

Incorporating Simple Pictures

If we have graphic capacity, it's relatively straightforward to display the lesson in a pictorial manner.

Figure 3.1 shows a seesaw upon which we may move the cursor in response to what the student wants:

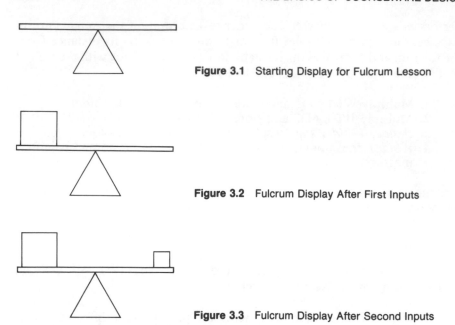

Figure 3.1 Starting Display for Fulcrum Lesson

Figure 3.2 Fulcrum Display After First Inputs

Figure 3.3 Fulcrum Display After Second Inputs

1. DISPLAY "How far from the center do you want your first weight placed?"
2. ACCEPT input and store in variable *position1*
3. Move cursor to *position1*
4. DISPLAY "How heavy is the first weight?"
5. ACCEPT input and store it in *weight1*
6. DISPLAY a square of size *weight1* at *position1*

Given these two student inputs, the screen would now appear as shown in Figure 3.2. To reiterate, we have

1. Accepted input about a weight and its location.
2. Stored that input in two variables, which we then use to draw a weight on one side.[3]
3. Repeated the process for the other side, changing, of course, the variables to *position2* and *weight2.*

Figure 3.3 displays the result.

We now have the four variables we need to calculate whether or not the seesaw will be balanced. Next:

4. Instruct the master performer to multiply the weights and distances and display the results.

---

[3] One way to show the weight is to have *weight1* as an input to a square-drawing program that tells the program how big a square to draw. *position1* is an input that says where the square should be drawn. We also could have included a small program that would permit students to move the cursor themselves, keep track of how far it had gone, and display the distance to them before they committed themselves to that one place.

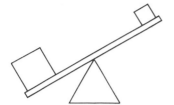

Figure 3.4　The Effect of a Greater Weight

Of course, we can do other things. For example:

> Display a graphic of the heavier side touching the ground by taking our original picture and redrawing it to show the effect of placing the weights where the student wanted them.
>
> Have the student try again with the same values but new distances (or the other way around).
>
> Get altogether new values and repeat the demonstration.
>
> If the numbers didn't create a balance, give the weight or distance that would have.

BEYOND DRILL AND PRACTICE: A WHOLE LESSON

The fulcrum example illustrates that there is no compelling reason to limit generative courseware to drill. We can, for example, design a complete lesson by integrating the calculations with a tutorial. We might start off with some introductory text, display a fulcrum, then a beam, and then two weights in balance, as shown in Figure 3.1. From there, we can show what happens when various combinations of weights and distances are combined, either by randomly generating values or by drawing upon a prestored set. Next, we can give students some direct experience choosing weights and distances of their own. And finally, if we had any doubt as to someone's mastery of the concept, we could offer drill-and-practice or a quiz. We might even include a program to act as a calculator that the student could use to do the multiplying.

AN EXAMPLE USING LANGUAGE

To this point, the generative courseware examples have all been based on numbers, but we can use generative courseware in teaching language skills. Difficulties arise, however, because human understanding of natural language depends in great measure on understanding the context in which words are used. A famous example of this is the expression *fruit flies:* according to the context, we're either speaking of insects or making a statement about bananas, perhaps, traveling through space. A native speaker of English would have no trouble comprehending the expression in context, but we would have problems building a master performer that could

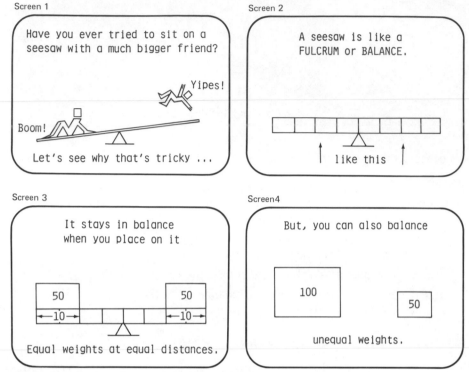

Figure 3.5 Sample Screens for a Fulcrum Lesson

understand in the same way. One could write a special routine to figure out every single occurrence of *fruit flies,* but that can't be done for any and all other such ambiguous statements.

Still, there are certain things in language which can be dealt with adequately by generative CAL. For instance, another famous example from linguistics is "*Green ideas dream furiously,*" a sentence which makes grammatical, if not semantic, sense. What we recognize in it is a pattern—a noun phrase followed by a verb phrase (or, if you will, a subject followed by a predicate)—that holds for many, many English sentences. (Indeed, a sentence that doesn't follow the pattern is said to have been "transformed" from a "kernel" sentence that does.) We can use this basic pattern and its extensions to develop a master performer for a lesson that teaches the various parts of speech and what linguists call "grammaticality."

WHAT A MASTER KNOWS ABOUT SIMPLE SENTENCES

We begin by providing the rough equivalent to the master performer's knowledge that $1 + 1 = 2$ or that $W1 \times D1 = W2 \times D2$. Here is a model of a simple sentence (that is, one with a single main clause):

SUBJECT	I I	**PREDICATE**		
DET I ADJ I NOUN	I I	VERB	I DET	I DIRECTOBJECT
The I big I boy	I I	hit	I the	I ball

The subject of this sentence consists of a determiner, an adjective, and a noun. The predicate, meanwhile, consists of a verb, another determiner, and a direct object. So in "The big boy hit the ball" each word fills a particular slot in a particular order.

There are, of course, a great many variations on this pattern (verbs that don't take direct objects but link the subject to the predicate, nouns without adjectives, plurals rather than singular determiners, and so on), but once we have identified a specific pattern, we can fill its slots by inserting a word that is a member of the appropriate class (determiners, adjectives, and so on). In fact, a game based on this principle asks players to supply a random assortment of verbs, nouns, and adjectives, which then get placed in what soon becomes a delightfully silly story.

We fill the slots by selecting words at random. Here is an example of what we might do. First, we create a stock of words for each class.

1 Create a variable called *nouns* and place into it: man boy ball dog cat roses tomatoes noses.
2. Create a variable called *determiners* and place into it: the a an.
3. Create a variable called *verb* and place into it: hit ate watched.

With this done, we randomly select one member from each list we have:

4. Create a variable *number* by using the random number function.[4]
5. Select word *number* from the *noun* list and place in *nouninsent1*.
6. Repeat this process and create variables *verbinsent, detinsent,* and *nouninsent2*.
7. Display these variables in this order: *detinsent nouninsent1 verbinsent nouninsent2*.

The results of running such a program vary each time because the constituent parts will be different, just as the numbers in the subtraction lesson differed each time. Using the words in our lists, we might get

The man hit the ball

or

The tomato ate the man

The output can be as varied as the number of words in each of the classes and the number of slots to fill in each sentence. But the design principle

---

[4] Where possible, it's more efficient to do this without creating a variable for the number.

remains: Given a way of getting values, we manipulate them in predictable ways. And this, of course, is precisely what we've done in the subtraction and balance examples above, using numbers instead of words.

GENERATIVE CAL FOR TEST BANKS

Rather than creating a list of nouns and verbs, we can create a bank of questions about a particular subject. Then, using the random number generator, we can choose items from this bank for testing students. The output can either be sent to the screen as the student completes a lesson or to a high speed printer to turn out enough tests for a whole class. Many schools have teams create a large bank of questions to produce individualized examinations. However large or small the application, the logic—selecting items from a central bank at random—is the same as selecting verbs or nouns from a list. The activities section at the end of this chapter provides you with such an exercise.

AN EXAMPLE FOR TEACHING MUSIC

As a last look at how we can use generative CAL, let's outline a lesson that teaches sight reading. Of course, music and computers have been used together for quite some time, and it is certainly possible to do things far more sophisticated than what we'll write here.

You first have to draw the staff and treble clef on the screen. You should also be able to position the cursor so that you may place a note—indeed a group of notes—precisely where you want it on that staff. To keep things simple, limit yourself to just a three-note melody picked from the eight notes of the middle octave, starting at middle C. First create the variable that will act as the bank of notes you'll draw upon:

1. Store C D E F G A B in variable *notes.*
2. Generate a random number N up to 7.
3. Select the Nth note from *notes* and store in *noten.*
4. DISPLAY *noten* at *position1.*
5. Repeat for the other two notes, displaying the notes and adding to *noten* as you go.

The screen should now look like the display in Figure 3.6.

Now ask students to enter what three notes they think are on the screen:

6. Display "What are three notes on the screen?"
7. Accept input and store it in *answer.*

Next, analyze the student's answer and make your decision about what display comes next:

Figure 3.6 Starting Display for Music Lesson

8. IF the *noten* matches *answer,* display "That's right" and stop.
9. IF *noten* does not match *answer,* display "That's not right" and stop.

You can, of course, do more:

If two of the three notes in the student's answer are correct, say so.

If all three notes are there but in the wrong order, say so.

If your system has sound, you can play back the student's answer along with the right one.

Include chords (groups of notes sounded together) or add the rest of the 12-tone scale or more octaves.

Teaching music—even a small part of it—uses the same logic as before. We:

1. Generate values (here, by using the random number function to select notes from a prepared list).
2. Keep a record of what we've done.
3. Present the visual form of that to the student in the form of notes on the staff
4. Accept and analyze the answer.
5. Take an instructional decision either to remediate or go on and give morc.

SUMMARY

Generative courseware goes beyond simply matching what the courseware designer programmed into the computer against the student's answer. It uses the capacity of the computer to create and to solve problems that we then give to the student. The computer's solution is compared to the student's, and the results in turn lead to a decision about what to display next. The great advantage of generative courseware over scripted courseware is that a very large number of examples can be written using a relatively small number of instructions. We merely repeat the instructions as often as necessary, and new problems and their answers are forthcoming. And as we have seen, we need not limit ourselves solely to mathematics; lessons in the social and natural sciences and humanities can also be created. With generative courseware we require a way of getting a set of values (from the student, from ourselves, or from generating them randomly) and a way of manipulating those values in predictable ways.

EXERCISES

1. At your computer, write a brief lesson that generates two random numbers, asks the student to add them together, compares the answer to the correct one, and then says if it's right or wrong.

2. Extend Exercise 1 by saying by how much the answer was wrong if that is the case. Repeat this with subtraction and multiplication problems, making sure always to display the larger number first.

3. Rewrite these two lessons so that the student can control how many questions you ask and how big the largest number will be.

4. Write a simple exchange that teaches and tests Ohm's law. Use the formula

$$R = V/I$$

where R is resistance, V is voltage, and I is amperage. Even if you are not familiar with the theory itself, you still should be able to give the student two values and ask for the third. Also try variants of this using $V = R \times I$ and $I = V / R$.

5. Try the fulcrum problem as outlined before, at first giving the student three values and asking for the fourth. Make sure that the number you generate will be such that this last answer will be a whole number.

6. Incorporate pictures into Exercise 5.

7. Generate some values for the accounts receivable and accounts payable of a small company. Ask the student to determine whether or not the company is showing a profit. There are clearly many other kinds of "PLUS" and "MINUS" situations; adapt your program's introductory remarks to one of your own choosing.

8. Extend the sentence generator by creating displays that use plural verbs with plural nouns.

9. Extend it again by using this sentence pattern:

DETERMINER NOUN LINKING VERB ADJECTIVE

Linking verbs are verbs that relate to the five senses (for instance, "taste" or "smell"), special verbs like "appear" and "seem", and the verb "to be." An example of such a sentence might be "The elephant was pink."

10. Create a bank of ten multiple-choice questions. Use the random number generator to select one and then present it to the student. Repeat this exercise, but display five questions, tallying the score as you go along.

11. If you're familiar with basic statistics, try this medium-sized project: Write a lesson about "variance"; that is, how widely a group of scores is dispersed around their mean. The four basic steps in finding the variance of a group of scores are

a. determining the mean (or average) of the group;
b. finding by how much each number deviates from the mean;
c. squaring the deviation of each;
d. calculating the mean of the resulting squared deviations.
   Begin by supplying some brief explanatory remarks about variance ("Variance is a measure of . . . "), and then ask the student to enter a group of scores. Explain each step as you perform it.

chapter 4

The Thinking Person's Pencil: Incorporating Graphics into Courseware

IN THIS CHAPTER

■ A successful graphic should be an integral component of an instructional design, not an add-on. It should have a clearly articulated purpose in the overall instructional plan.
■ Like graphics in other media, courseware pictures can clarify, concretize, and entertain. They can also make the computer into an interactive, intelligent pencil that responds to what students want to see. Successful courseware graphics include ones that
   • draw geometrical shapes,
   • plot functions on graphs,
   • tabulate information,
   • demonstrate ideas in perception and problem solving
■ Two basic design principles should guide courseware graphics:
   1. Make the abstract concrete.
   2. Use the computer as an intelligent device that does the drawing as the user does the thinking.

WHAT YOU SEE MAY BE ALL YOU GET

A picture may be worth a thousand words and still not do enough. At least, that's so when we merely add graphics to courseware, rather than incorporate them. The instructional role of graphics in courseware needs to be as clearly defined as that of any other element in a lesson. Add-on images—happy faces, exploding spaceships, and the like—may catch the eye but they

Figure 4.1 Little Engine

won't engage the mind. Moreover, we make poor use of computers if the pictures we show with them are no different from images in textbooks or, worse, simply vaguely conceived embellishments somehow intended to motivate. Only when we exploit the interactive nature of computers can we see what makes courseware different from other instruction.

This is not to say, of course, that a graphic cannot be there just to delight. But it does mean that the computer, unlike any other media except the live teacher, allows—indeed demands—interaction. Not to use that interaction undercuts many of the reasons to use courseware in the first place.

NOT ALL LITTLE ENGINES CAN

Many lessons display impressive graphics, which is not surprising when one considers what professional programming achieves in almost every home arcade game. What is less impressive about much courseware graphics is how often they are poorly thought out in terms of their role in the lesson. Figure 4.1 is an all-too-representative example.

Give it a right answer, and the little train chugs off, carrying its little load of little happy faces. In Figure 4.2, the apparent price for failure is having your spaceship blow up; the real price for failure may be having to watch this each and every time you miss an answer. Not all courseware behaves this way—thankfully—but much does.

Figure 4.2   Crashing Spaceship

Too often, we can't identify the purpose for all the colors and shapes as a student tries to learn except that they're merely there. Again, nothing is wrong with looking at an attractive display; but a graphic in a lesson should be there to solve a very particular instructional problem for which we think a visual image is the best solution. The question to ask when we incorporate graphics in courseware is this: What are we trying to accomplish at this point in our lesson that best can be served by a picture?

MAKING THE ABSTRACT CONCRETE

A major function of any graphic in any medium is to render the abstract concrete. That is, many concepts can be more readily understood by a kind of incarnation, a bringing to the senses of what might otherwise be available only as an idea. For instance, we are going to consider a number of abstract statements like "The square of a binomial equals the squares of its two parts plus twice their product" or "We not only see, we look for." For most of us, these general ideas are not immediately evident, and we would benefit greatly if some visual analog were present. Figure 4.3 presents such an analog.

It shows that if A and B are two numbers—any two—then the areas of the two squares labeled A^2 and B^2 added to the areas of the two rectangles labeled AB all fit within an area drawn by adding A and B together and squaring the result. We'll come back to this in greater detail shortly, but it's clear that the drawing neatly makes the rather cumbersome point that "the

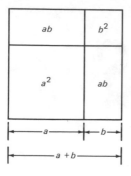

Figure 4.3 $(A + B)^2 = A^2 + 2AB + B^2$

square of a binomial consists of the squares of its two parts plus twice the product of the two." Even seeing the same thing expressed algebraically—$(A+B)^2 = A^2 + 2AB + B^2$—doesn't make for as quick an understanding. The graphic makes an enormous difference.

BEING TOLD WHERE TO LOOK

Is the mere presence of the drawing enough for students to grasp the relationships between the sizes of the different squares? If that's so, we certainly don't need courseware. We are touching a rather critical point: If a drawing in a book can teach effectively, how different will it be to display that same drawing in a CAL lesson? For unless we believe in some mysterious electronic force, why should we expect that any better results will follow simply because students see drawings on a screen instead of in a book?

THE INTELLIGENT PENCIL: INTERACTIVE GRAPHICS

Rudolf Arnheim (1969) remarks that Jean-Jacques Rousseau would not believe $(A+B)^2 = A^2 + 2AB + B^2$ until Rousseau himself had drawn the figure.[1] That suggests an important caveat about courseware design. Although the computer may do the actual drawing—that is, physically create the images—it should do so as a surrogate for students' hands, not their minds. What gets drawn should be what the student thinks should be drawn, only far more neatly and far more quickly. The source of the instructions about what to draw must remain resolutely human.

Who would argue that thinking rather than drawing is at issue? Well, judging by the number of exploding space ships and happy faces, many designers. Their faith in the power of computer technology apparently extends to believing that merely showing a picture on a computer screen

---

[1] Arnheim notes sadly that whole generations of students were taught the equation without the figure, thereby depriving them of a powerful and simple demonstration of why it's true. This is not to argue that having the graphic, we don't need the math. The two complement each other.

makes people learn. But that's not the case. A courseware graphic must do things that are first and foremost important instructionally and that can't be done as well by any other medium. That's the importance of interactive graphics: no other medium so gracefully turns ideas to images.

DRAWING WITH THE RIGHT SIDE OF THE INTELLIGENT PENCIL

What might be in a lesson to teach the equation about squares and binomials? We could begin with some written explanation, followed by a drawing. Different colors could highlight the different shapes. We could show the smaller shapes in one part of the screen and assemble the whole in another part, displaying the appropriate messages as we go. This goes beyond a book, to be sure, but it isn't much different from TV or movie animation that also uses color and motion.

However, if we add the element of interaction, courseware comes into its own. A drawing stays on the printed page and is the same for every reader. An animated cartoon adds motion and sound, yet it too remains the same for every viewer. But—if we are clever enough—students can direct a CAL lesson to draw pictures at different times and in different ways so that each session reflects their own understanding. Just as each user differs, so will each session.

In the rest of this chapter, we'll look at examples of lessons that use interactive graphics. Throughout, we'll be directed by these guidelines:

1. A visual image renders concrete and accessible what may be otherwise abstract and difficult.
2. Courseware graphics must be more than the static images of books or even the animated images of film: they must be interactive.
3. Using the computer as an intelligent pencil provides students with visual analogues of their thinking. The computer substitutes for their hands, not their minds.

One last note. This chapter presupposes only that you have access to relatively simple graphic facilities with which to design lessons. We won't discuss sophisticated techniques, such as rotating three-dimensional shapes or using computer-aided design packages. Neither will we look at the various graphic programs (such as *MacPaint* and its clones) that let us draw for the sake of drawing. None of these is really intended to be used within tutorials but instead stands on its merits, quite apart from the question of contributing to courseware.

SQUARES WITHIN SQUARES

Let's design an interactive lesson to demonstrate that

$$(A + B)^2 = A^2 + 2AB + B^2$$

In rather difficult and awkward English, the equation states that the square of a binomial consists of the squares of its two parts added to twice their product. Because students who would be introduced to this aren't likely to have trouble with the concepts of squares and rectangles or the necessary math, we'll make use of these knowns to teach what is not known, that is, the truth of the equation. We start with the usual introductory general remarks, but they, of course, aren't interactive. So we will then ask students to provide us with two numbers. In this way, the basis for the demonstration will come—at least in part—from them. The pseudocode looks like this:

1. Display brief introductory remarks along with a request for a number.
2. Accept input, and store in variable *numa*.
3. Position cursor in lower left quadrant of the screen.
4. Store cursor position as variable *possq1*.
5. Draw square using *numa* as input to a square drawing program.[2]
6. Label square "A^2."

We might encounter a practical problem in the size of the number we'll use to draw the square. Anything too large will take up the area we need for the rest of the graphic and anything too small won't be visually effective. We have to experiment with various sizes, and when we determine them, we'll include limits on the size of the number we will be asking students to provide. This done, we then repeat the same instructions, asking for a second number.

7. Display request for a second number.
8. Accept input and store number in variable *numb*.
9. Position cursor in upper right quadrant.
10. Store position as variable *possq2*.
11. Draw square using *numb* as input.
12. Label square "B^2"

To complete the first stage of instruction, we need a third variable to draw a pair of equal rectangles, which will be as long as *numa* and as wide as *numb*:

13. Multiply *numa* by *numb* and *store* the result in variable *numab*.
14. Position cursor in upper left quadrant.
15. Store position as variable *posrect1*.
16. Draw a rectangle using *numa* and *numb* as inputs for length and width.
17. Label rectangle as "$A \times B$."
18. Position cursor in lower right quadrant.
19. Store position in variable *posrect2*.
20. Draw a second rectangle, again using *numa* and *numb* as inputs.
21. Label rectangle as "$A \times B$."

[2] The instructions assume you have "square-drawing" routine that takes a number as input and draws a square of that size. You also need a way to record the cursor's different positions.

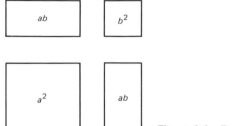

Figure 4.4 Four Shapes That Equal $(A + B)^2$

Figure 4.4 represents the screen as it would now appear. If possible, we should fill each shape with a different color. If we have a monochrome display, we could draw a different pattern for each shape. Either addition will make the shapes easier to distinguish later on.

To recapitulate:

1. We have drawn four shapes—two squares of different dimensions and two equal rectangles—using the student's own numbers to determine their sizes.
2. We have placed them in the four quadrants of the screen along with the appropriate comments about each.

At this point, we could remind the student that this lesson is about $(A + B)^2 = A^2 + 2AB + B^2$ and that the screen display demonstrates this. To show the first part of the equation, we need simply draw a large square using the sum of the student's two numbers as input:

22. Add *numa* and *numb* and store in variable *numc*.
23. DISPLAY explanatory text.
24. Position cursor in middle part of screen.
25. DRAW square using *numc* as input.
26. DISPLAY explanatory text.

The explanatory text in these lines should say that this larger square represents the left side of the equation, $(A+B)^2$; that is, the numbers the student gave us that we've added together and then squared. We could go on and solve the equation, substituting the student's own numbers but we won't right away. Instead, we'll incorporate the graphic. Since the equation is true, all the other shapes on the screen will fit within the large square $(A + B)^2$. To make the process become more interactive yet, we'll highlight the smaller shapes and let students pick which one they want to move.

27. DISPLAY request for student to choose one of the four smaller shapes at the corners of the screen.
28. ACCEPT input, *store* result in variable *pos*.
29. Place cursor at *pos*.
30. Erase shape.

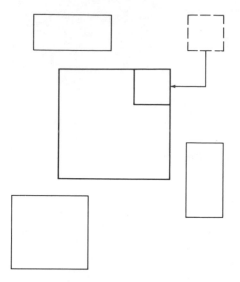

Figure 4.5 Moving a Small Shape into Position

31. Position cursor within large square.
32. DRAW shape within square[3]

The result of these lines is that a shape goes from its initial position to a new one within the square. Figure 4.5 shows this. We repeat the instruction for each of the four shapes, letting students choose the shapes they want moved. It's convenient to start by setting the cursor at the bottom corner of the big, center square. This gives a reference point for placing everything else. You'll have to experiment with finding the arrangement that is best for your system.

There are a number of extensions to this simple program that can make it even more interactive:

Let the student choose not only which shape to move but where in the larger square to place it. (A system with a light pen or mouse would be ideal here, but labeling the square and letting the student move the cursor to a starting point for each shape also works.)

Repeat the program in its entirety with different numbers, showing the generality of the proof.

Begin with a straightforward demonstration using preselected numbers before letting students pick their own.

The demonstration can be repeated as many times as students need. The generality of the proof emerges as new numbers produce the same result, the small shapes always fitting within the larger one. Moreover, the

---

[3] If your system permits, you can replace the last three steps by just moving the smaller square at the edge of the screen to its position inside the larger one.

movement from abstract numbers to concrete objects has been controlled by the learner, both in choosing original numbers and in positioning the shapes. The equation is no longer just a collection of symbols, perhaps a seemingly arbitrary one at that, but a description of a world students can see and manipulate.

AN EXAMPLE WITH GRAPHS: PLOTTING FUNCTIONS

Lessons that teach plotting can also let students use computers as intelligent pencils and so make abstract ideas concrete. Students often think an equation like $y = 2x$, for example, is just a collection of symbols without much real meaning. Their understanding can change, however, when they can create a visual analogue and see the relationships the equation expresses. Look at Figure 4.6, for example, to see how the curve changes when the equation changes.

A Cartesian grid, of course, is the standard way of presenting these relationships. Typically, classroom exercises have students locate places on the grid and join them. A computer lesson can do this and more. The computer takes over the purely mechanical operations, letting the student concentrate on the concepts being taught.

THE BASIC FORM OF A PLOTTING LESSON

For this task, the first requirement the courseware must meet is a graphic system with a Cartesian grid and a way to mark a point anywhere on the screen. The x and y axes themselves should be always visible. In addition to common mathematical operations (adding, subtracting, multiplying, dividing, finding squares and square roots), a system should also be able to translate a string of input into an equation that the system can solve (that is, it knows what to do with $2x$ in $y = 2x$). We'll need this capacity when we ask students to enter their own equations.

The lesson can begin with a demonstration that generates a set of values to satisfy a sample equation, plots the points on the screen, and then

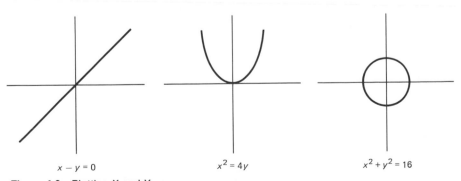

$x - y = 0$ $\qquad\qquad\qquad$ $x^2 = 4y$ $\qquad\qquad\qquad$ $x^2 + y^2 = 16$

Figure 4.6 Plotting X and Y

joins them. Using the example of $y = 2x$, the bare-bones design of the program works this way:

1. Let x equal 1.
2. Solve the equation for y using this x value.
3. Place a dot at x,y.
4. Increase x by 1.
5. Repeat steps 2-4 n times.

If we were doing this by hand, we would create a table of xs with corresponding ys:

If x equals   1 2 3 4 . . . -1 -2 -3 -4
Then y equals   2 4 6 8 . . . -1 -4 -6 -8

The pseudocode looks like this:

1. Create variable *dots* equal to the number of dots to be drawn.
2. Create *count* and set it at 0.
3. Create x and set it at 1.
4. Create y equal to two times x.
5. Place dot on screen at point x,y.
6. Increase *count* by 1.
7. If *count* is greater than *dots,* stop.
8. Increase x by 1.
9. Go to step 4.

The screen should look like Figure 4.7 at this point. Here are a few ways this lesson can teach:

Begin with some expository material, followed by a list of possible relationships between x and y (y three times as big, half as big, and so on).

Be an "articulate expert," that is, one which explains what it's

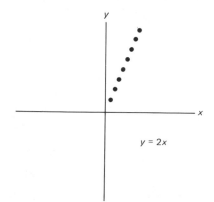

Figure 4.7 Plotting $Y = 2X$

doing as it calculates the various values of x. For instance, it might say:

> "x is now 5; therefore, y is two times that or 10; here is 5 on the x axis; here s 10 on the y-axis; and here is where they meet."

Test the ability to solve the equation by withholding the answer until students give theirs.

Add a mini-lesson on finding various locations on the two axes, making use of a pointing device (like a mouse, lightpen, joystick, or cursor keys).

Let students enter their own equations. (This requires some means of translating standard mathematical notation into your system's legal statements.)

Display several curves on the screen simultaneously, perhaps in different colors, to make different relations clear. These relationships need not be linear or straight-line; using squared numbers will produce various kinds of parabolas.[4]

You will want to try various extensions to the program: how much to teach, how sophisticated to make your error diagnosis of the student, and so forth. All this has to be specified in your instructional design plan. Throughout, you'll use the computer to do the mechanical work of finding places on the graph and drawing lines, thereby letting the student see concrete representations of the relationships that the abstract equation expresses.

GRAPHS THAT TABULATE INFORMATION

One of the most frequent uses for graphs is to summarize large amounts of information. The implicit relationships among a group of observations are much easier to grasp in graph form than as a series of numbers. We understand and absorb ideas quickly because the graph presents the essentials with the least possible irrelevancies. This is, of course, true for any good graphic, be it in book, film, or courseware. But once again, it's the potential for interactive graphics, for letting the student decide what the computer will show, that gives courseware an advantage over the other media.

Suppose we are designing a series of geography lessons. In one, we might want to talk about the relationship between amounts of rain and optimum crop yield. In another lesson, we might want to talk about the movement of people from one part of the country to another. In a third, we might wish to see temperatures for a series of days. As long as the necessary information is available, a bar graph can depict the numbers for any period the student chooses and do so at any point in the lesson.

---

[4] The limiting factor here probably will be the resolution of your screen. With large numbers, the dots are placed too far apart for a pattern to emerge; if the numbers are too small, the computer will round them off and place too many dots on top of each other. You'll have to experiment a bit to see what works best.

We will need a means of drawing an *xy* axis, labeling it, and drawing rectangles for the bars themselves. For the graph to show temperatures for a period of days, for example, our pseudocode will be this:

1. Draw *x* and *y* axes, but label only *y* (since we don't know yet how many bars we need to draw).
2. Ask how many days to be plotted and store as variable *bars.*
3. Divide length of *x* axis by two times *bars* and store in variable *unit.* (This allows us extend our display over the whole length of the *x* axis. We need twice as many units as bars so that the spaces between the bars will be as wide as the bars themselves.)
4. Create variable *count* and set it at 1.
5. Position cursor 1 *unit* to the right of the *y* axis.
6. Ask student for the value of this bar (that is, the temperature for this day) and store in variable *value.*
7. Draw bar so that its height is equal to *value* and its width is equal to *unit.*
8. Label bar.
9. Position cursor 1 *unit* to the right of bar.
10. Increment variable *count* by 1.
11. If *count = bars,* stop.
12. Go to step 6.

In step 4, we set *count* at 1 to keep track of the number of times we have to repeat asking for student input and drawing a bar. We increment *count* by one after each bar, checking to see if it equals the total number to be drawn. If it does, this part of the program ends; if not, the program loops back to get more student input. The positioning of the cursor each time makes sure that both the bars themselves and the places between them will be spaced equally. Figure 4.8 represents a display showing average temperature for ten days. If we were showing the effect of rain on crop yield, it would be straightforward to do two graphs and place them side by side. Again, the computer has not done anything that students couldn't do for themselves but has done it more quickly and probably more neatly.

WE NOT ONLY SEE WE LOOK FOR

Let's now look at an image that makes the point that people don't just passively respond to what's in front of them but actively seek out patterns. This idea is, of course, common enough in the study of perception. Most people have seen the chalice that may, in fact, be two faces in profile or the cube that seems to lie one way and then the other (see Figure 4.9).

The same kind of drawing can make the point that our ability to solve problems suffers when we don't see what's in front of us but instead impose our preconceived notions. Look at the diagram in Figure 4.10. At first glance, most people will see an arrangement of rectangle, parallelogram, and two triangles. If you were to ask someone to reproduce the drawing, there might be some considerable measuring and figuring. However, another

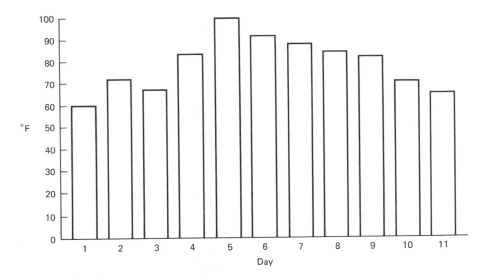

Figure 4.8 Bar Graph Showing Daily Temperatures

look reveals that it is, in fact, a pair of equal but overlapping right-angle triangles. The graphic is a good demonstration of the problem of whether or not we see what is there or project our own expectations. By making the drawing part of an interactive lesson, we can make the point more clearly.

A CAL lesson to show that we look for patterns before we see any might begin by displaying the drawing already in place and asking students to count the number of shapes they see. It's important, naturally, that the initial presentation doesn't direct students to any particular part of the drawing; otherwise, the idea will be lost. That's probably best done by having students point with a light pen or mouse, but they could also point

Figure 4.9 Two-Way Chalice

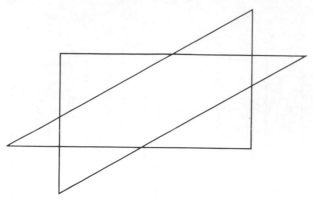

Figure 4.10   Two Right-Angled Triangles

with the cursor or enter numbers that correspond to one of the five smaller shapes. The program could go forward, simplifying the drawing, until at last the two large overlapping triangles that make it up would be shaded in, one at a time. Of course, the program is only a simple demonstration that doesn't warrant being much more than one part of a longer lesson. But its interactive nature—letting students input in some way what they see—makes the lesson on computer very different from the static picture in a book or even an animation where what's seen is decided solely by the designer.

SEEING SQUARES

We can make this point with the diagram shown in Figure 4.11, adding a practical demonstration about problem-solving. With this drawing on the screen, we ask students to indicate how many squares they see, coloring each as it's pointed out. Most people quickly recognize that in addition to the small squares, there are squares formed by grouping four adjacent ones,

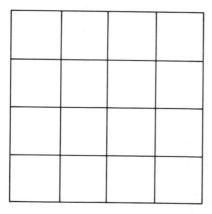

Figure 4.11   A Square with Many Squares

either at the corners, in the middle, or at the center. And most students usually remember to count the outside square, the one that contains all the others. The difficulty lies in forgoing the obvious two-by-two groupings and seeing three-by-three ones. Until students show this (by pointing to the squares on the diagonal or by listing numbers of various squares), the program gently nudges them in the right direction. Allowing students to enter which groupings they see and letting the program respond to that affords interaction that demonstrates the need for flexibility in problem solving.

SUMMARY

A graphic should be incorporated into a lesson, not just added on as an afterthought. It should have a clearly articulated purpose in the overall instructional plan. Courseware drawings can clarify, concretize, and add enjoyment, but, beyond this, courseware can make the computer into an interactive, intelligent pencil that responds to what the student asks to be drawn.

EXERCISES

The following exercises are mid-sized projects that will take about five to ten hours of work at the computer:

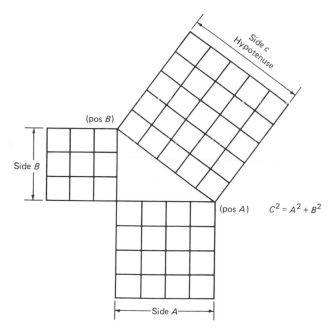

Figure 4.12 Pythagorean Theorem Screen

1. Design a lesson that teaches Pythagorean theorem: "The square of the hypotenuse in a right-angle triangle is equal to the sum of the squares of the other two sides." Begin with a program that draws a right-angle triangle using student input. Place restrictions on the size of the input so the drawing will fit on the screen. You'll also need a "square-drawing" program that draws a square which itself will be made up of 1-unit squares like this. The basic graphic you'll use should be similar to that shown in Figure 4.12.
2. Design a plotting lesson that lets students enter their own equations. This requires translating the standard mathematical notation into your system's "legal statements." As far as possible, the student should enter the equation the same way it's written on paper. Prompt students to enter each side of their equations and check for legality (in terms of your system) before going on.
3. Design a lesson that uses any kind of data consisting of a series of observations over a period of time (like sales, goods consumed, or populations). Use a bar graph to represent numbers the students enter.
4. Ask the student for a series of numbers. Use it to design a graphic demonstration that shows what the median in a list is (that is, the number that comes midway in an ordered series of numbers).

REFERENCE

Arnheim, R. *Visual Thinking* (Berkeley: University of California Press, 1969).

chapter *5*

Necessary Details: The Craft of CAL

THE CRAFT OF CAL: ADDING THE FINAL TOUCHES

The other chapters in this book try to ask "big" questions about designing courseware. What follows here, however, is a series of small answers about fine tuning a lesson after the fundamental planning and initial coding have been done. Designing courseware is a combination of theory and craft—perhaps even art. That is, in addition to theory-based assumptions about such stuff as the attributes of master performers or ways of representing students, there is a series of techniques making up the pragmatics of writing courseware that is easy for students to use. Since learners have much to think about just trying to understand content, we want to do as much as we can to ease their negotiating through the lesson itself.

CALCRAFT: FINE TUNING COURSEWARE

Calcraft (to coin a word) is often just common sense, especially after someone has pointed it out. The best way to learn calcraft is to pick it up from a variety of sources—other designers, good programs, complaints from users, trial and error. Incorporating the techniques we'll look at comes only when we fine tune a program that's already substantially sound. A poorly conceived lesson with poorly explained ideas won't benefit from the best of calcraft. But a good lesson can only get better.

SERVE THE USERS

The basic dictum we follow in calcraft is to serve the users, not have them serve us. Many programs tend to be written by people who are programmers first and educators maybe, a situation that often results in lessons that ignore what humans must contend with when they interact with machines. Students are used to live teachers, and they also know how to look at books. But even sophisticated computer users require some practice with a new program before they can stop worrying about its operation and begin thinking about its purpose. Courseware designers, like other software producers, have to reduce the load on students so that they can concentrate their efforts on learning the ideas being taught, not on figuring out how to make the program run.

We should also remember that even if we aren't going to turn over complete control to learners, they nonetheless have a right to control some things. They can set their own pace, review what they need, get help when they ask, and be sure about what we expect them to do. We are not merely being "user-friendly" when we do this but promoting their (and our own) success. It's to both our benefits to make their lives as simple as possible.

BULLET PROOF THE LESSON

A bug-free program is the user's first right.[1] It may seem self-evident, but we should never release a program that hasn't been thoroughly tested. We may not be able to guarantee that we have found every bug, but we can commit a good part of our time to trying. It upsets students to get cryptic messages of the sort that say that they have made an "Illegal Call to a

---

[1] "Bug-free" in this context refers to a lesson's code. Naturally, courseware should be free of other sorts of bugs too—wrong information, typographical errors, and the like. It is both surprising and appalling how many programs don't take the necessary care.

Function." They haven't made a call to anything; we have, and we must test the program often enough so that nothing the student does later on can cause such things to appear. This is, of course, quite different from the problem of responding to errors students make when they try to understand content.

TESTING THE CODE: COPING WITH MURPHY'S LAW

A trap to avoid when we test for programming bugs is the "best-case scenario" where we look only for obvious bugs or run the lesson assuming our knowledgeable selves as the end user. As we code the lesson, we have to anticipate real students and how they might crash the courseware. Any computer program, of course, can be defeated by someone intent on doing so. But we must assume good will and make sure that well-intentioned students have a program that runs as advertised, without crashes or bugs that take them where they don't want to go.

PROVIDE A STATUS LINE

Once we are reasonably confident that the code runs properly, we can fine tune the user interface. We start by asking ourselves what students need to know at any point and then telling them. We can do this by reserving a status line, a place on the screen for messages about the lesson's logistics. Such information isn't about content but about running the lesson itself.

The most convenient place for a status line is usually at the bottom of the screen, leaving the rest of the display for what we teach. Regardless of its position, however, the status line should be in the same place every time; a student should never have to search for it from display to display. Arrows, reversing background and foreground colors, or blinking characters all can highlight or call attention to parts of the status line's messages, as they can elsewhere in the lesson. Overusing these effects, of course, diminishes their effectiveness. A whole screenful of blinking words or garish colors induces eyestrain, not learning. Figure 5.1 gives some sample status lines.

The messages on the status line should be straightforward: how to get help, how to exit, how to review, and so forth. But other messages can be relayed too. If the program is slow at a particular spot (perhaps because it's loading a file from disk or doing a time-consuming check of input), it should say so: "Please wait—I'm loading a file." It's disconcerting for students to think the lesson has abandoned them or crashed when they are really waiting for it to finish doing something.

Status line information also differs from reports of scores ("You've scored 68 percent") because the status line is about operating the program itself. (Moreover, people don't want to be told every minute how they're doing, except perhaps in a game.) The purpose of the status line's message is to tell users where they are and what they can do next—go to Part 1 or try Question 5 or whatever—so they can feel in control.

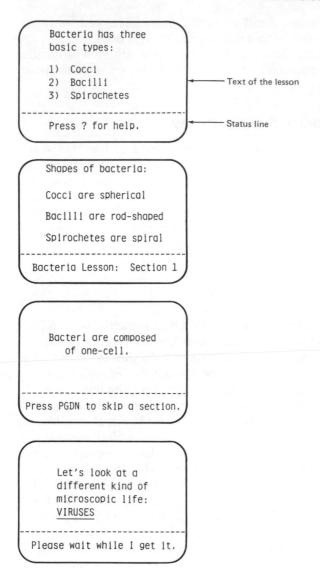

Figure 5.1 Sample Status Lines

ECHO INPUT

Another way to make sure that users always know what's going on is to echo what they input. Learners don't appreciate hitting a key and seeing nothing apparently happen, as might well be the case when the student's answer requires the system to do something time-consuming. Even when we know the computer can respond immediately, we should still give students a chance to see what they've keyed in so that they can edit out errors. In general, seeing what they enter is a signal to students that they are at least doing the right thing operationally, even if they aren't giving the right answer.

ACCEPT INPUT THE SAME WAY ALL THE TIME

Just as we can reserve a place for a status line, we can reserve the same general location on the screen for student input. Again, we don't want them to waste energy hunting for the place where their answers should go. As Figure 5.2 indicates, positioning the cursor provides a visual cue.

For example, on fill-in-the-blank questions, we move the cursor to where the answer will appear when it's entered. A math question in which the sequence of operations moves from right to left should position the cursor position accordingly after each digit is entered. Multiple-choice questions should use a consistent layout for each question, its choices, and the place for the students to enter an answer.

DON'T COMPLICATE THE STUDENT'S INPUT

We shouldn't ask students to do our coding for us by entering 1s for YES and 0s for NOs. Similarly, if we want them to answer *yes* or *no,* they shouldn't have to enter anything more than a Y or N. We can go still further and make the most likely answer a default value; that is, we can let the user either choose to enter it explicitly or just hit the carriage return. Hitting the carriage return (or *ENTER* on some machines) becomes the equivalent to choosing the first option listed. In Figure 5.3, for example, the Y is the default

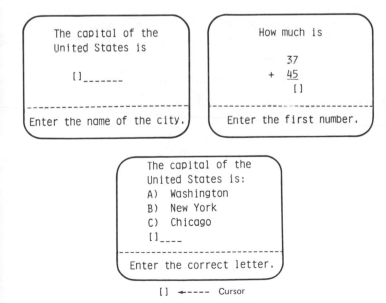

Figure 5.2 Positioning the Cursor

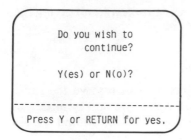

```
      Do you wish to
        continue?

      Y(es) or N(o)?

----------------------------
 Press Y or RETURN for yes.
```

Figure 5.3   Using a Default Setting

value, and hitting it or the RETURN key has the same effect. This reduces the load on the user since RETURN is faster to find than the Y key.

USING FUNCTION KEYS

Another way of easing the load on students is to use the function keys found on many computers. These keys can be programmed to accomplish in one keystroke what otherwise might take several. For example, if you provide an online glossary, the user could access it first by going to a HELP menu, then to the glossary, and then to the particular term. However, a function key can combine the first two keystrokes, speeding things up. Similarly, keys can be reserved for exiting the program, reviewing material, or skipping forward.

Again, the hallmark is consistency. Using the same key to do the same thing each time enables students quickly to find help menus, end lessons, review ideas, try quizzes, and so on. Messages on the status line or help menus can say what each function key does. Somewhat more cumbersome than displaying messages, perhaps, would be to make a template that fits over the keyboard and says what the special keys do (see Figure 5.4).

ASKING FOR AND EDITING THE STUDENT'S RESPONSE

If we require student input to take a special form (like having no commas in very long numbers), we should say so at the outset of the lesson and issue reminders at the appropriate times. The same is true for rounding off numbers: A diligent person might give an answer to four decimal places and be counted wrong if the program were expecting only two.

Help	F1	F2	Quit
Skip	F3	F4	Review
Take quiz	F5	F6	Glossary

Figure 5.4   Sample Template for Function Keys

Better than telling the student to do any of this is to include routines that edit responses before we analyze them. Such routines can silently accomplish the following tasks:

round decimals or fractions into integers
remove commas
set the number of decimal places
substitute numbers for letters like 0 for O or 1 for l (common mistakes for computer novices)
ignore extraneous characters (like dollar signs)
substitute *and* for ampersands

MORE COMPLEX RESPONSE EDITING

Looking for Key Letters

More complex editing allows us to accept partially correct spellings by looking for key letters in key positions. For instance, we might specify certain letters as wild cards. Anything in those positions would be ignored and the answer read as correct if the other letters were in the right places. This lets us go beyond searching for only exact matches. For example, designating * as a wild card and *D*G* as a right answer means that any of DIG, DOG, or DUG would be correct. In the same way, "P**CE" would mean that any one of PEACE, PIECE, or PEICE is correct, thereby forgiving the poor speller. Programs for younger children benefit especially from this sort of response editing.

Looking for Keywords

Key-letter checking also can be extended to keywords. For example, we can say that as long as a word or its acceptable alternative appears anywhere in a response, the answer is right. We therefore would take any one of *kilos, kilograms,* or *Kg*, regardless of what else is there (*I think the answer is 100 kilos*). We could also specify, perhaps, that although we'll take any one, it must come after the number *100*. We could even accept the equivalents of *100* and *kilos, kilograms,* or *Kg* in pounds or ounces in some (admittedly infrequent) cases. The pseudocode for the first part look like this:

IF *answer* includes *100* and (*kilograms* or *kilos* or *Kg*) and *100* comes
    before (*kilograms* OR *kilos* OR *Kg*)
THEN *answer* is correct

By combining a search for key features (or their acceptable synonyms) with their positions in an answer (*before, after, first,* or *last*), we can do very complicated analysis in a single pass. We can continue in this manner looking for several features in the sentence in various configurations.

ALLOW STUDENTS TO EDIT THEIR OWN INPUT

There are limits to how much we can edit responses, but we can also let users edit their own. We've already discussed why we should echo input and let students see what they've done before we accept it. Most of the time, we shouldn't use a procedure where analysis begins as soon as a single key is struck (as we might do when accepting a Y or N). Students need the control to enter what they want, look at it, and fix it if necessary before they hit RETURN. For long entries (like whole sentences), we might even explicitly have the status line ask users to check that what they've typed is what they really mean. (Overdoing this can slow down and annoy students; they should be allowed to disable this feature whenever they want to.)

THE LESSON HAS TO BE ROBUST TO BAD INPUT AND ILLEGAL ANSWERS

Forgiving as we may be through response editing and by letting students themselves check for errors, we have the final responsibility to spot "bad input," which is not the same as looking for a wrong answer. Bad input is an illegal response. Here are some examples:

>
> a number instead of a letter (like 1 for l)
> a letter that's out of range on a multiple choice question (like "R" on where the choices are only A through E)
> a carriage return when we expected a letter, number, or word
> a function key at the wrong time
> an unanticipated word

Usually all that's needed in these cases is a short statement about the acceptable range and type of answer ("Please give me a number") and a repetition of the question. But we can also record how many times this happens; students who consistently give bad input may be either confused, trying to quit, or mildly malicious. In any case, they won't learn much at this session and we should intervene. Three times and out with bad input is a good rule of thumb. This rule is not, however, a tutoring strategy that says how many wrong answers the student can make on any given question.

KEEPING THINGS CLEAR VISUALLY AND SEMANTICALLY

No designer deliberately produces an unclear explanation, either about content or operating instructions. But what is clear and self-evident to an expert probably won't be that way to a novice. In general, we have to imagine what our audience's background has been, anticipate their level of understanding of how the lesson behaves, and try to accommodate it. If we know the target population well, it will be straightforward enough to determine the appropriate level of the lesson's discourse, that is, its vocabulary and sentence length. But if we don't know, we need to find out, either by speaking to people who do, consulting books on reading levels, or, best of all, trying out the lesson with typical users. We have to concern ourselves with two kinds of clarity:

>
> visual clarity: how things look on the screen
> semantic clarity: what things mean

We have two ways of improving both:

> planning screen organization *before* and *during* design
> field testing *after* we have coded the courseware

VISUAL CLARITY

Keep Screens Simple

A cluttered screen is a chore to read and a puzzle to decode. We can unclutter screens with the following techniques:

- Use lots of white space to separate units of thought. This provides a visual cue to where one idea stops and another starts.
- Avoid solid blocks of text. Most computer displays are difficult enough to read without crowding together words, even logically related ones.
- Keep sentences relatively short and readable; that is, avoid convoluted instructions or peculiar words.
- Write shorter sentences and paragraphs than in ordinary, discursive prose.
- Make sure character fonts are fairly large and legible.
- Choose contrasting background and foreground colors that won't strain the eyes.
- Don't break words in odd places and wrap them around to the following lines.
- Don't overuse highlighting techniques such as changing colors, fonts, inverse video.

Figure 5.5 provides some examples of good and bad screen displays.

Windows

Windows are used increasingly in commercial software to organize displays. A window is an area of the screen dedicated to a single purpose, such as presenting one type of information, showing graphics, or inputting answers.[2] Figures 5.6 and 5.7 will give some examples.

> A window can be a scratch pad in a math lesson where a student does calculation or practices; the other windows can display problems, give hints, or accept the actual responses.

> A window can show the effects of changing an object while keeping the original in view. We can have one version of a sentence in one window, for instance, and also show what it might look like after a certain kind of revision.

> For teaching computer programming, we could show code executing in one window and its listing in another.

---

[2] True windowing allows for more than one program to be run at the same time. That isn't possible for most microcomputers, but we can still run different parts of the same program at different screen locations.

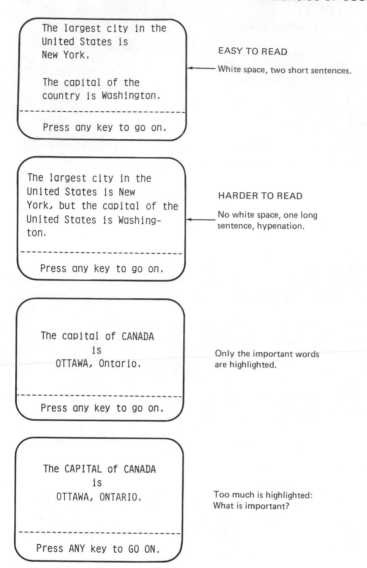

Figure 5.5 Making the Screen Clear

One window can display a formula and a second can display the effect of substituting different values into it.

ORGANIZE BY PAGE

Computers can display text either by scrolling or paging. Scrolling means we add new lines at the bottom of the screen and bump up everything else one line, with the top line disappearing altogether. This can lead, however, to unrelated information being mixed on the same screen, which in turn leads to messy visual displays and murky instructions.

```
┌─────────────────────────────────────────────────────┐
│  ┌─────────────┐        ┌─────────────┐              │
│  ¦   Solve:    ¦        ¦ Enter your  ¦              │
│  ¦             ¦        ¦  answer:    ¦              │
│  ¦45612 / 875  ¦        ¦  []  _____  ¦              │
│  └─────────────┘        └─────────────┘              │
│  You can use the computer                            │
│  as a caluclator here:      Use                      │
│  ┌─────────────────────┐    C:  for calculator       │
│  ¦                     ¦    A:  to give answer        │
│  ¦                     ¦                              │
│  └─────────────────────┘                             │
│ ─────────────────────────────────────────────────   │
│  C -- Lets you use the computer as a calculator.     │
└─────────────────────────────────────────────────────┘
```

Figure 5.6 Windows in a Math Lesson

Paging, as the word implies, displays information a whole screenful at a time. We can, if we wish, show a page all at once or reveal it section by section; but either way, when one entire logical unit is completed, the screen clears and new stuff appears. This helps keep related units together. Refer to Figure 5.8 for the difference between scrolling and paging effects.

Paging also has two other advantages:

Letting Students Review: Self-pacing, after all, means more than just going forward when one wants; it also means going back to check something. Many computers have keys like "PgUp" and "PgDn" which can be programmed to let a user flip through material, segment by segment.

Letting Designers Revise: When a designer is producing a courseware lesson, a page makes for easy reference. It's a lot easier to find "Page 1" on a print-out than "The fourth major

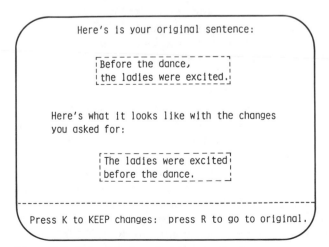

Figure 5.7 Using Windows in a Punctuation Lesson

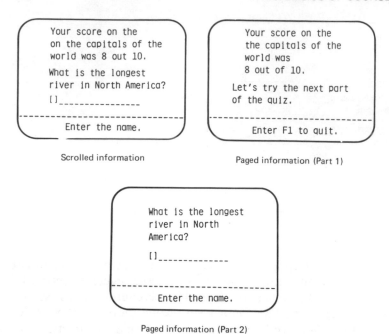

Scrolled information   Paged information (Part 1)

Paged information (Part 2)

Figure 5.8   Organizing by Scrolling or Paging

export of China is. . . . " We can also label a page in the bottom
corner as we design the lesson and remove it later in the version
we release.

USING STORYBOARDS

One way of helping ourselves to think in terms of pages is to use a
storyboard. This standard device of script writing consists of a series of
sample screens that show what various displays will look like when students
will see them. Displays can be arranged and rearranged until we find their
best sequence. Figure 5.9 shows a sample storyboard.

A note of caution: A storyboard doesn't show the underlying assumptions or workings of the program—the knowledge representation scheme,
the student models, and so forth. It shows only the endproduct that the
student sees. As a way of organizing material, a storyboard is useful since it
can provide a template which, once designed, ensures that every display
includes the important components: explanation, place for student response,
status line, and so forth. It also helps produce a layout of the screen more
clearly.

However, a storyboard tends to lock us into script-based courseware.
Because storyboards are very convenient when writing branching, frame-
based programs, that kind of lesson sometimes appears inevitable. We
should resist using storyboards if they lead us towards seeing courseware
only as electronic programmed instruction, turning to Board 64 for answer

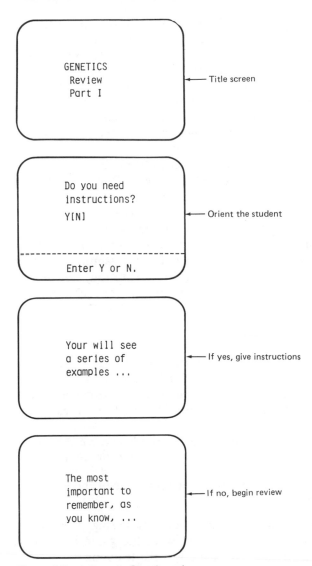

GENETICS
Review
Part I
← Title screen

Do you need
instructions?
Y[N]
← Orient the student

Enter Y or N.

Your will see
a series of
examples ...
← If yes, give instructions

The most
important to
remember, as
you know, ...
← If no, begin review

Figure 5.9 A Sample Storyboard

A and Board 87 for answer *C*. At the very least, we first have to demonstrate that our subject is best taught that way. That said, storyboards are helpful in clarifying our thoughts in the early going or showing what the endproduct can look like.

FIELD TESTING

In addition to merely hoping that what we've designed is visually and textually clear, we must test its clarity by trying out the lesson with typical future users. Eventually, of course, we'll want to know if our lesson teaches effectively, and we'll do a "summative evaluation" where we will statistically analyze the scores from large groups. But during development, we also need real users drawn from the target population to judge whether our language and screens are clear, information is missing, or the lesson is hard to run. Rather than use formal evaluation methods, we sit down with volunteers and let them go through the lesson while we make notes, mental or written. We look for the places where they struggle to decipher what the lesson wants them to do or what the content means.

A problem at this stage is getting users to be frank. Frequently, they try very hard to please by assuring us that all is well. Our problem is to convince them that they are not being tested but that the lesson is; we'd like them to be friendly but firm critics. During a formative evaluation, we should interrupt the lesson only when absolutely necessary. We won't be there in the real world, after all. When we find ourselves having to explain what the lesson really means or else saving it from crashing altogether, we've found a place to revise. That's cause for celebration, not despair because seeing what needs to be improved is the purpose of such formative evaluation.

USING THE COMPUTER IN FIELD TESTING

Another kind of field testing calls on the computer itself to gather information about how the lesson runs: where the trouble spots are and what works. Informal notes taken during field testing are valuable, but we can also build in information-gathering routines. For instance, we can keep track of

> how many times the HELP facility gets accessed (and which parts)
> what percentage of students miss what questions or do poorly in specific sections
> how much time students spend on various portions of the lesson
> where crashes occur

We must insure, of course, that like any record-gathering process, the measures themselves don't intrude. We don't want the gathering of data about how well the lesson operates to slow down the teaching.

USERS ARE THE BEST JUDGE OF THEIR OWN PACE

A common problem in much courseware is how fast to go. There's no reason to assume, of course, that everyone will take the same number of seconds to read a display. Therefore, delaying the system an arbitrary number of seconds will only frustrate those who need more or less time. A simple pause routine with "PRESS ANY KEY TO GO ON" in the status line lets the student exercise control over the courseware's pace. We need merely pause (not stop completely) the lesson and then start it again when any key is struck. Again, consistency is the watchword: We can choose either RETURN or "PRESS ANY KEY" or anything else but should stay with it and its placement on the status line.

THE RHETORIC OF COURSEWARE

The rhetoric of courseware concerns choosing not *what* we'll say but *how* we'll say it. "Gee-whiz" attitudes about computers may be disappearing as more people use them more, but it's still worth underlining that students have to deal with machines, not humans. Computers aren't people—people are. If we obscure the artificial nature of the interaction, we raise expectations which, when they go unmet, raise hackles. In general, if you assume a live and intelligent human being at the other end and write the computer's part of the dialogue accordingly, you won't say anything on the computer that you wouldn't say face-to-face. The following guidelines help:

Don't sound omnipotent   Unless you've done an extraordinary piece of programming, your lesson will exercise only partial control of the learning process. Don't mask that with an omnipotent tone that is neither honest nor likely to induce sympathy should things go awry. Don't take a tone of disembodied computerese—the machine as Big Brother—and say things like, "I cannot compute those parameters."

Courseware does not have to project omniscience. It can convey the message that learning is a cooperative effort in which machine and human each will do what it does best. For instance, the chapter on tutoring strategies shows that it's possible to let students make some important decisions about things when the machine can't (like figuring out the meanings of words). We can also let the user—even children—indicate what's going on, help us make decisions about where next to go, and tell us if they understand. The image of the computer as an all-knowing intelligence isn't appropriate for courseware.

Don't be coy   Coyness takes several forms. It can be the contrived excitement of a "SUPER!, *name variable*, YOU'RE BRILLIANT." After someone has had ten tries at an answer, this just becomes insulting. Restrain pseudohuman imitations, such as breathless exclamations either of delight or disappointment. If you wouldn't praise someone extravagantly for something in person, don't do it in courseware. A simple "Right" or "Sorry, think about . . . " does it, letting students draw their own conclusions about how brilliant they are.

Never abuse   Above all, never abuse a student with "Dummy" or "Only a real fool would miss that." It's frustrating enough to get something wrong without being laughed at by an anonymous sadist safely speaking through a pile of silicon chips. The first time this kind of "wit" happens, it may be mildly amusing (although probably only to the writer). After that, it just annoys. In general, be careful with jokes; few things are as deadly as a gag done to death. Try for a light and friendly tone, one that won't call attention to itself.

Avoid pseudodialogues   Be careful with pseudodialogues of the sort where you ask questions you never intend anyone to answer (for example:

"Can you explain to me why this happens?"). It is legitimate to ask the student to think about an issue and discuss it later with a teacher or friend. But unless you are really ready to deal directly with a response, a question like that promises more than courseware can deliver.

Some programs, in the name of discovery learning, even mislead the student into thinking something might work and then play dumb: "Oh, I guess that won't do it—let me try it this way." That's distorting the real nature of the computer, poisoning future wells of credibility.

Using the student's name   You should try, of course, to individualize messages to students by trying to understand their understanding. This is genuine individuation, not merely arbitrarily invoking the variable where you've stored the user's name. However, when you do use the name variable, you can place it just before you have something particularly important to say: "The thing to remember, *namevariable,* is. . . . " Dozing students perk up noticeably when they see their names in lights, as it were.

Respond to the way the lesson develops   Better than simply sprinkling someone's name throughout the lesson, you can individualize instruction by shaping your responses to how the student is doing. When students miss a few attempts on a question and then succeed, you can speak to them accordingly ("No, that still isn't it." and "Now you've got it."). This involves extra programming, but if the records kept by the student model are going to be useful, they can make a start on real individualizing—courseware's avowed aim.

Keep bells and whistles under control   The temptation with a new toy is to play with it. As we saw in the chapter on incorporating graphics, however, vaguely thought out graphic embellishments are dubious. Fancy graphics should be kept for situations where they are demonstrably the best way of explaining something. Drawings that are elaborate and clever—merely clever—slow down a lesson and take a lot of memory. That they do or don't motivate is an experimental question. Certainly, a screenful of blinking images in garish colors can't help someone concentrate. In the same vein, sound effects should be used sparingly to really get attention or show something particular (as in a music program, for instance). Like pictures and jokes, sounds can quickly intrude to bore or annoy. Waiting thirty seconds for "Hail to the Chief" to finish playing on a tinny speaker will hardly please or motivate anybody, except perhaps the programmer.

GIVING HELP

Help can be of two sorts:

1. *Clarifying lesson operation,* as in how to
   Get in and out of different parts of the lesson
   Try quizzes
   Skip sections

Review
Get progress reports about scores and skills
Finish up the current session

Some of this information can appear on a status line, but if too much does, the status line itself might need a status line. It's better to have the status line (or perhaps the template on the functions keys) say how one can get this information, rather than always trying to provide it.

2. Guiding the student to extra explanations of subject matter:
    glossaries of difficult terms
    mini-lessons for remediation
    reviews
    exercises for extra practice

By structuring a lesson into self-contained units, portions of the basic instruction can be recycled. You can branch the student back to an explanation that's already been given once before, a technique that saves having to rewrite the same information several times. For example, the display that introduces a term can itself be an entry in a glossary. However, you might instead decide that an explanation that's failed before will continue to be inadequate; in that case, you'll need to present a different version of the same idea.

Menus

Menus are especially useful for leading students to HELP of both kinds. Figure 5.10 will give us a few simple examples. The status line that's displayed in the normal course of the lesson can tell the student to enter "HELP" (or perhaps just "?"), which in turn will cause a menu to be displayed. That menu itself can branch to other, more specific help menus, which can lead to still others. A more complex strategy is "context-sensitive help" which responds to a request for help first by seeing where the student is in the lesson and then presenting a menu focused on that location. This gets students what they need quickly, without their having to search through a mass of irrelevant information.[3]

If HELP will extend several levels deep into the menu, it's also a good idea to give experienced users a way of getting directly to where they want to be without going through all the menus. This can be done by accepting complex forms of input which are equivalent to several help commands entered sequentially. But that's an extra; we should first design a reliable and consistent set of basic help menus.

As with other parts of a lesson, the student should go through the same format asking for help every time. To repeat, students have enough on their

[3] When we design menus, we can reduce the load on the student still more by highlighting each choice in a menu (with inverse video, for example) as the cursor moves from one topic to another. When students see the topic they want highlighted, they select it by pressing RETURN.

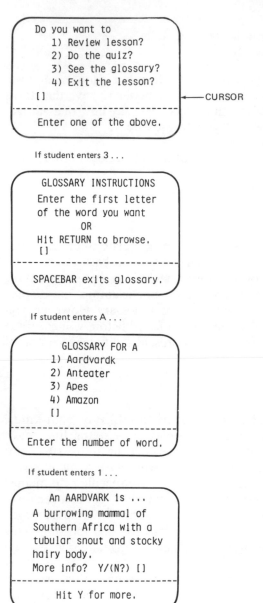

Figure 5.10 Using Menus

minds just learning a subject; they should not have to make a major effort to get help.

Manuals

Manuals are another important source of help, often overlooked or added as hasty afterthoughts. Good courseware has good manuals for both student and teacher, both of whom are consumers of a product and have a right to know about it before they use it.

The Student Manual   Before they try to use a lesson, students should have

> a statement of how the lesson fits their goals
> an overview of the lesson
> a good sense of what they're expected to do
> instructions for getting the lesson running

Providing printed manuals doesn't mean that we neglect online help, or simply duplicate it, for that matter. The two kinds of information are quite different:

> Online help gives information about the immediate problems of running a lesson or the specifics of subject matter.
>
> Printed manuals explain why someone should spend time with the lesson and then how to start.

A manual, then, is not a warmed-over version of the courseware or a substitute for the hands-on experience of actually using it. It is a way of getting students to want to get their hands on in the first place.

The Teacher's Manual   No less important is a manual for teachers that tells them more than how to get the student started. A teacher's manual is a statement from one professional to another:

> It first situates the courseware within the curriculum, saying what it can do and how it should be used.
>
> It makes clear the instructional strategy. We don't have to give away any proprietary secrets, but we must talk about the medicine we're marketing. Like an ethical drug company speaking to a doctor, we say when and how to use the product and when not to.
>
> It provides information about hardware and overall logistics.

Maintenance Manuals   A third kind of manual (and most often neglected) is one for ourselves or whoever else will have to maintain the lesson. Documentation about the logic of the programming is critical if we hope to revise it in the future. Comments are best placed in a printout (or some private version of it) where we can set out what each segment of code does, as we write it. We should also make the logic of the program control explicit. It is entirely common for a clever programming trick to be a complete mystery a few weeks after it was written, which makes revising sometimes impossible. A comment in the code is a cheap investment.

A FINAL WORD

If there's a theme that runs through Calcraft, it's respect for the user. Courseware is a product and deserves the same scrutiny as any other. Shoddy, poorly conceived work deceives more than just the school that purchases it. It cheats students of their time and efforts. But it's also bad for other designers: Each time a piece of courseware fails to live up to its promise, it compromises the credibility of the profession. We can't, of course, regulate the quality of courseware except by making sure the marketplace knows its value. But we can regulate ourselves.

SUMMARY: A CHECKLIST FOR CALCRAFT

Bulletproofing the Lesson

Is the program free of all known bugs?

Have you tried the worst-case scenario?

Providing a Status or Message Line

Is the status line in the same location all the time?

Does it give necessary information about running the lesson at different times?

Does it say when there will be a delay?

Does it say how to get help, review, exit, etc.?

Giving Help

Is HELP available about how to
  Operate the lesson?
  Skip or review sections? quizzes? reviews? Get scores? Quit?

Is there further explanation of material in the form of glossaries? exercises? mini-lessons?

Can content be recycled as help?

Do menus direct students to context-sensitive help topics?

Are help menus given in a consistent fashion?

Can experienced users go directly to help without menus?

Accepting Input

Is input echoed so that students can see what they've keyed in?

Does the program appropriately prompt users to check their input?

Can students edit their own input before it gets analyzed?

Does the program request input in a consistent way?

Does input for the same things go in the same screen location each time?

Does the cursor move to where the answer will appear?

Are there default settings for the most probable responses?

Does the lesson ask students to do its coding (e.g., asking for 1 or 0 instead of "Yes" or "No").

Editing Input

Does the program silently edit
    Substituting letters for numbers (O for 0) P?
    Substituting numbers for letters (1 for l)?
    Rounding or changing decimals and fractions into integers?
    Ignoring extraneous characters (like $,0,etc.)?
    Setting the number of decimal places?

Can the program perform checks on
    Key letters?
    Key words?
    The same answer for more than one key word?
    Key words located in different places in the answer?

Is the Lesson Robust to Bad Input and Illegal Answers?

Does the program branch back to the appropriate place when there is bad input such as
    a number instead of a letter (like O for 0)?
    a letter that's out of range on a multiple choice question?
    a carriage return when the lesson expects a letter, number, or
        word?
    a function key at the wrong time?
    an unanticipated word?

Does it keep track of how many times bad input is entered and then take appropriate action?

Does the Lesson Use Function Keys?

Are function keys available whenever they can save the student keystrokes?

Are function keys available to
    Get help?
    Skip or review a section?
    Take quizzes?
    See glossaries?
    Quit the lesson?

Are function keys used in a consistent way?

Keeping Things Clear

Is the screen laid out with lots of white space?
Are sentences relatively short?

Are there no solid blocks of text?

Are no words broken or wrapped around to the next line?

Are character fonts readable?

Do background and foreground colors complement each other and make for readability?

Are various highlighting effects used judiciously to direct the student's attention?

Is the level of discourse appropriate?

Is the Lesson Organized by Pages?

Is unrelated material always kept separate on the screen?

Can pages be used to allow
the student to review material?
the designer to revise?

Are users allowed to judge their own pace?

Can the user set the pace at which he'll see material?

Is the program consistent in its PAUSE routine?

Can windows be used
As scratch pads?
Display problems?
To give hints?
To accept the actual responses?
To show the effects of changing an object while keeping the original in view?

Field Testing

Has the program been tested with users drawn from the eventual target population?

Do formative evaluators know their role is to criticize?

Have weak places in the lesson been identified and revised?

Does the Computer Itself Gather Information About the Lesson?

Can the program tell
Which questions most students miss?
Which HELP sections are most often accessed?
How much time students spend on the various parts of the lesson?
Where system crashes occur?

The Rhetoric of Courseware

Does the lesson
Avoid a tone of contrived friendliness or pretend humanity?

Assume a tone of omnipotence or affect computerese?
Speak to the user as if learning were a cooperative venture?
Explain what it's doing?
Avoid being coy?
Ask questions that can't be answered or conduct pseudodialogues?
Avoid abuse or sarcasm?
Use the student's name to get attention?
Individualize remarks on the basis of obtained results?
Reserve graphics and sound effects for when we can show they're genuinely needed?

Manuals

Does the Student's Manual tell students
    What the program will cover?
    Why they should be doing it?
    How to log on?
    More than just what's on the online HELP?
    Motivate students to try the program?

Does the Teacher's Manual
    Provide information about hardware and program logistics?
    Situate the lesson within the curriculum?
    Explain and justify the program's instructional strategy?

Does the designer's manual (or printout)
    Explain the programming flow and logic?

*chapter*6

The Start of a Grand Design—and Before

IN THIS CHAPTER

- We examine a set of broad issues that need to be addressed *before* we consider courseware solutions.
- We have to ask what problem we are trying to solve and what evidence there is that courseware is the best solution.
- To do this, we look at
    - the boundaries of what we will teach
    - what should be the outcome of instruction
    - what the current output is
    - what part of the present instruction accounts for the poor output
- Having identified an instructional problem, we ask
    - Do we need interaction?
    - Is interaction possible, given the availability of expert knowledge?
- We also consider the general issue of control in a lesson:
    - How much variety will we permit the student to show?
    - How will we cope with it?
    - What kind of information will we need to gather about the student?
    - How we are going to get it?
- And, finally, we ask ourselves
    - Who benefits from what we are doing?
    - Can we modify existing solutions to analogous problems instead of starting from scratch?

BEFORE THE BEGINNING

How do we begin to design courseware? Much of what is in this book deals with issues that are relevant only once we've already decided to use courseware: instructional design schemes, master performers, model notation, and the like. But before we even get to them, we need to think about the more basic questions of what problem we are trying to solve and why we think courseware is the best solution.

Most of the time, in fact, we should reject courseware solutions. The efforts and costs to produce courseware are high; there may be cheaper or faster solutions—and more effective ones, too. Failing grades, for instance, are not necessarily signals for moving lessons from textbooks to microcomputers. Such moves may change the delivery system but little else. So first we have to come to some understanding about the causes for the students' poor output. Only then can we begin to speculate about the possible benefits of adapting courseware to the subject matter.

THE SOLUTION IN SEARCH
OF A PROBLEM

If such advice seems obvious, let's again remind ourselves that when we design courseware, we face a particularly invidious danger: the solution in search of a problem. For the practitioner, it may be hard to resist the notion of the computer's omnipotence, hard not to think of courseware as *the* best solution to any student's failure. What we have to do instead is clarify the causes of failure by identifying the skills and knowledge that are missing. Having accomplished this, we will still have to prove (or at least make reasonably sure) that such skills and knowledge are taught best by computer.

For instance, the educational literature often says that the mere presence of computers in the classroom motivates students. It might follow then that using the computer will engage the attention of poorly motivated students. But poor motivation usually runs deep and reflects a vast network of emotional and intellectual values. Merely changing the delivery system won't make any difference unless we can show that other delivery systems *per se* are responsible for students not wanting to learn. The message otherwise stays the same, regardless of the messenger.

Alas, we have no exact algorithm to follow to prove that we should try a courseware solution. But there are some starting points, questions that must be asked before we think of design plans like those in Chapter 1. The questions that follow prompt us to think of educational problems as parts of whole educational systems, systems in which courseware is but one possible component. Obviously, these questions add up to an unavoidably imperfect process, but they can warn us about doomed courseware before we've committed too much of ourselves to withdraw gracefully.

IS THERE AN EDUCATIONAL PROBLEM THAT CAN BE SOLVED BY COURSEWARE?

What should be taught? This is a rock upon which many tall educational ships founder. Very often, when people tell us they have a problem, all they have is a vague feeling that something has not gone well. When a bridge collapses, we see dramatic evidence of a problem although its exact cause may be harder to find. There is seldom such dramatic evidence in schools.

A student's failure is an output of an educational system, a confluence of processes gone wrong. Determining which of them is the real culprit is a fundamental issue for the courseware designer. Our very first task is to identify what we're really concerned with, what we should teach. That in turn requires us first to establish the boundaries of the system we're interested in.

WHAT WILL BE THE LESSON'S BOUNDARIES?

A system's boundaries tell us where that system stops and starts. If we think about our cars, we might think about roadways, petroleum companies, traffic lights, or assembly lines. All contribute to our getting around, just as do the car's fuel system and our own vision system. What to exclude from consideration depends on what we're interested in at any given moment and what we can manage. For instance, if our car stalls on a freeway on-ramp, the real fault may lie with the auto makers's quality control; but our immediate concern is getting to safety and then home.

What Will Be Taught?

So too with courseware. Students may fail to learn because they come from broken homes, can't read, can't add, are bored, are lazy. But those things are part of the *environment* of a learning system, parts we can't manage, at least not in the way we can manage the set of exchanges between machine and student. We have to identify the area in which we are competent.

A lesson to teach American history, for example, can't simultaneously teach American geography, although the two are surely related. A program to teach BASIC string commands can't be about BASIC's matrix commands, despite the legitimate place of matrices elsewhere in the curriculum. A lesson in calculus can't also be about algebra, even though calculus students often fail because they don't have sufficient skills in algebra.

Who Will Be Taught?

Moreover, a program's boundaries have to distinguish not only among topics but among levels of users. Different users need different levels of discourse and different focuses, even though the basic material is the same. Consider students whom we say fail geography because of poor comprehension skills. That assessment makes the problem sharper than just saying they've failed geography, but the cause of failure still isn't evident. What do we mean by *comprehension* in geography, at what level does one need it for a particular lesson, and how does one develop it? Indeed, whose responsibility is it to teach? Previous grade levels? Remedial teachers? The classroom geography teacher?

So, while we can see real enough trouble—an instructional system to teach geography with a poor output—identifying the cause and the feasibility of redressing the trouble may be difficult. What sort of courseware will make a difference to a failing geography student? Is a computer better used to improve overall reading skills rather than geography in particular? How much of geography can be presented graphically, thereby making reading less critical?

IF THERE IS A PROBLEM, WHAT SHOULD THE SYSTEM BE OUTPUTTING?

When we say that a problem exists, we are saying that the end product of the system doesn't meet our expectations. Students, for example, may experience certain troubles with writing; their output should be good grades and, more importantly, good essays. Generally, clearing up writing problems falls to English departments. But literature teachers often can't teach basic composition and complete the literature syllabus too. Should writing, therefore, be taught across the curriculum, with each discipline teaching its own kind of writing? This has its own problems, not the least being that it's difficult to get people to articulate precisely the writing standards of their disciplines.

By contrast, it's easy to say that a bridge should be able to withstand winds of 150 miles an hour or that an astronaut should be able to dock a shuttlecraft with 100-percent accuracy. Most educational outputs are more difficult to specify. Can we always say what constitutes good style in writing and then set up standards appropriate to various grades? Can we always say how clear writing should be for a particular level and a particular discipline?

WHAT ACCOUNTS FOR THE CURRENT POOR OUTPUT?

This question gets us away from output and points us toward what is currently in the system itself. The answer begins with a list of components of the instructional system in which we are interested. As we've seen, we must first establish the boundaries of the system; that is, we have to declare a point beyond which we won't go. Within that perimeter, we need an inventory of the parts that are in the system.

Let's go on with the example of a system to teach writing skills. The poor output is a poor essay. The components of essay writing include such mechanical things as spelling, grammar, and syntax but also include reading skills and habits, vocabulary, logical thinking, motivation, organization, and clarity. What causes a particular poor essay?

Are the basic ideas there but awkwardly expressed?
Does the writer jump from topic to topic?
Are there lots of spelling and grammatical mistakes?
Is the writing listless, suggesting a lack of motivation?

Any or all can cause a poor essay. Designing a courseware solution first means determining the real causes of the poor output. Lessons in grammar won't help the sloppy organizer or the indifferent reader. Lessons in spelling won't help the student with problems in logic.

Of course, even if we find the cause of the poor essay, there is no reason to think courseware can help necessarily. Typically, writers of awkward sentences haven't thought through what they really mean. But no courseware has been developed with the natural language capacity to understand even the simplest utterances, much less the confusing ones of confused writers. Courseware can do little if students lack the self-discipline to paraphrase their own sentences as they revise (if they can't say what they mean, who can?). Similarly, students whose essay organization is poor have to be asked to justify the placement of each idea. "Thought-processers" can help, but it's still the individual who must reason out relationships among ideas, not the machine. There's not much reason to use courseware in these cases. The point need not be labored: We first have to identify the real causes of failure before deciding on a solution, courseware or otherwise.

DO WE NEED INTERACTION?

Having identified a problem and its cause, we ask whether the computer is the best medium to solve it. In Chapter 1, we saw that the primary difference between the computer and other delivery systems was the degree of their interaction. Unless we can show that interaction is really necessary for learning, we don't really need courseware. If, for example, we require mostly text, students can read books. If we need graphics—even with motion or color or sound—film will be enough. And if we are going to ask just "choose-one-of-the-above" questions, programmed workbooks suffice. Only when we go beyond these strategies to full-fledged interaction do we need courseware.

WHAT KIND OF EXPERT KNOWLEDGE IS AVAILABLE?

It is one thing to say that interaction is necessary and another to say it is possible. One reason why courseware design is difficult has to do with constructing master performers and student models. That human beings can do so many things so easily doesn't mean, of course, that those things are easy to describe. In fact, the opposite is usually true. How do children internalize the grammar of their language? How do ballerinas learn to dance "musically" as well as technically? How does a pitcher master a curve ball? Things like these we can describe only partially and often vaguely. Using a computer does not make these difficulties go away but makes them critical.

For how are we to change the behavior or otherwise control complex systems like human beings if we can't first unambiguously say what we want them to do?

Before we can consider courseware as an alternative to other forms of instruction, we must sit down with subject matter experts and have them tell us what the output of our courseware should be. Unless they can tell us explicitly, we don't have a good candidate for courseware. The very nature of the medium requires that we clearly articulate how we want the lesson to behave. If we can't do that, we're defeated before we begin and we'd better know it. There are many important topics in a curriculum, of course, that can't be explicitly described. They are better taught in the traditional way— whatever its defects—than by a halfway competent computer lesson.

STUDENTS AS LEARNING SYSTEMS

Students are parts of instructional systems too, of course. Thinking of people as systems isn't new. We speak of their cardiovascular and neuromuscular systems, their legal and economic systems, and their religious and cultural ones. When we identify some entity as a system, we mean

> it's made up of things
> those things are organized in some way
> they interact with each other
> they have an output

Although we may be able to speak of a single output of a system, most systems we are likely to think about, be they spacecraft or six-year-olds, represent a terrific amount of complexity. And that makes it an especially complex matter to guide them into producing some single, desired output.

In a learning system, we can expect a large number of topics and subtopics, types of learners, and tutoring strategies. If all that any of them could do would be to assume just one of two states, it still would be a considerable task to describe the whole system at any given moment. But students can do more than simply know or not know a subject the way that a light switch is on or off. They can try many methods for solving a problem, make many sorts of mistakes, and need many kinds of explanations. The possible number of states an instructional system can take can be huge. When we design courseware, therefore, we have to identify the range of possibilities—Topic A is known at Point B to Student C but Skill D isn't— so we can say where to intervene.

HOW MUCH VARIETY WILL WE ALLOW THE STUDENT TO SHOW?

Students are quick to learn some things, slow at others, prepared or unprepared. During the course of a lesson, they could dutifully enter A, B, or C, or something we've never thought of. From a welter of possibilities, we can deal only with a limited number, yet we still have to be sensitive to the potential range of possible responses. If we aren't, we distort the image of the student. The issue is control.

CONTROL IN EDUCATION

In the popular imagination, the word control conjures up vast banks of soulless machinery in the service of the biggest possible brother. But the word need not threaten since we control things all the time. We keep our cars from going wherever fate, fortune, and the laws of motion might take them. We keep our two-year-old's hands away from danger. We keep ourselves from another helping of pie. Naturally, we do have to separate the act of control from its moral legitimacy. The assumption in this book is that a courseware designer has already answered the moral questions and is ready to consider technical ones.

Since the Second World War, a rich body of ideas about the control of whole systems has grown up that has application to a wide range of disciplines, including education. Perhaps our first reaction to this might be to say that people are not machines. That is the point, however; people are vastly more complex than our most sophisticated machines, and if we are to teach them anything, we need a way to approach that complexity.

HOW WILL WE COPE WITH THE COMPLEXITY OF STUDENTS?

The usual way that teaching systems keep from breaking down is by limiting the number of possible choices allowed the student. This is familiar elsewhere. No restaurant lets you eat anything you want but instead reduces your options to what the chef will prepare. No school lets students take any course they want either but reduces options by insisting on a curriculum. And no courseware can let any user do anything or ask any questions at any time.

However, successful systems can also exercise control by extending their own range of responses and ability to react to many things. Think of two persons playing chess: Whatever move one makes, the other must be ready for it or the game is over. It's not possible, to be sure, to arrange things so that everybody in every lesson has every choice. Good teachers try their best to get close to this ideal situation, but what they actually provide is a livable mix of cutting back on complete student choice and extending their own ability to respond. Like good teachers, courseware designers have to decide how much to limit students and how much to try extend the lesson's power to respond. In concrete terms, this means specifying the nature of input that the lesson can handle, be it single-key responses or complete ideas, freely expressed.

WHAT DO WE NEED TO FIND OUT ABOUT THE STUDENT?

Extending a lesson's range of response also requires information about what is going on in a student's mind. Briefly put, information is what decreases uncertainty. Let's think of driving a car: The only way we can get from here to there without getting maimed is by having information coming in that reduces our uncertainty about where roads go, where a truck may suddenly stop, where unfinished bridges abruptly end. Without all that, the system of us and our car becomes increasingly unstable (we careen into a truck) until the system is no longer viable (we're dead). Successful systems make available lots of information: not just data, but data with meaningful patterns. Successful teachers know not only their subjects, but also their students, and they model their students' minds and adjust the teaching accordingly.

Successful courseware is similar in function and intent. The purpose of a student model, for instance, is to reduce uncertainty about how well the learner is doing. We need this information not merely to assign a grade but to tell the computer what material is best suited at any given moment. If we don't know, the distance between what is needed and what is offered increases and the situation becomes more and more unstable. If things get bad enough, there will be a complete breakdown. So as part of the courseware design process, we have to decide upon a way of modeling the student to collect the necessary information. We need to ask

What do I want to know about the student?
How am I going to get it?

Educational systems do not neatly circulate information. A single reading (say an exam score) is a crude measurement when we have to decide what to do next. Therefore, courseware designers must specify where a lesson will collect information, what sort of information it will collect, and the use to which that information will be put. That first requires a deep sense of what the lesson teaches and the kinds of possible misunderstandings. If we don't know, we might as well leave the whole business to chance. We need answers to the following:

Is it Concept A or Concept B that's not understood? Or indeed Subconcept A–1?
Where do students deviate from the master performer?
What specific bug do they have?
What questions are answered poorly by one particular student and by others?

From the very start of the design, we want to think about ways to gather this information. We want to know what students might do or say that could lead us to infer what they know or don't know.

WHO WILL BENEFIT?

This question often gets to the center of things. Whose values are being served? For whom is this worthwhile? A lot of grand schemes fail because the people they touch do not value them and so will not be a part of them.

The users of courseware, both teachers and students, must be brought into the process and understand how the proposed teaching will benefit them. For if the benefits of a proposed lesson don't match the needs and wishes of its potential clientele, the result will be like a falling, unwatched tree in the forest: interesting but irrelevant.

The best way to ensure that users share our values is first to know those values ourselves and then explain them to others. Certainly, students need to know more than just how to log on; they need to know why they should try the lesson and what they can realistically expect of it. Teachers have to know where in the curriculum the courseware fits and what strategies are being tried. Having to articulate this to other people helps us clarify our ideas about what we're doing.

DOES WHAT WE'RE TRYING TO DESIGN LOOK LIKE ANYTHING ELSE?

Reinventing the wheel wastes energy. It is important that we look for analogies between what we're trying to do and systems already proven successful in practice. If parallels exist, perhaps we can copy solutions. We can at least inquire what other courseware is available—and not just on the subject we're teaching—discovering those approaches that we might modify to our purposes. Can we borrow their architecture? Appropriate their techniques? It goes without saying that we respect copyright and give credit where credit is due.

SOME LAST WORDS ON GRAND DESIGNS

The questions that follow are intended to probe the instructional system only in broad terms and see the underlying organization and outputs, the ways that things interrelate and interact. None of these questions can provide anything like sufficiently specific advice about what to code or what lines of reasoning to follow for specific courseware. But to ignore them is to forget about the necessary wholeness of a lesson, the interconnected complexities of student, subject matter, and machine. It is not some vague, idealistic feeling we are invoking here but a hardheaded reminder that we forget at our peril.

SUMMARY: A CHECKLIST FOR PRELIMINARY DESIGN

Defining the Boundaries of Your Goal

What is the extent of the instructional problem you are trying to solve? What should the educational system of interest be outputting that it is not now? What expectations aren't being met?

What accounts for the current poor output? What's there now and what's there that's breaking down? How does the delivery system affect things?

Why is the goal worthwhile? What are the goals of those being affected (students, instructors, administrators)? Who will benefit from your proposed solution? Whose values are being served?

Can you find a problem typical of the class you wish the student to be able to solve (or give samples of typical skills or knowledge your lesson will teach)?

Providing a Formal Statement of Objectives

What is the target population?

What are the ages, grades, and skill levels of those who will be taught? What are their backgrounds, handicaps (if any), and assumed entry levels?

What kind of information will you collect about the way they experience the lesson? How will you collect it? What kind of student model could you use?

Determining CAL as the Medium of Choice

Why is interaction necessary? What kind? Could your lesson be delivered by another medium without loss of effectiveness or an unacceptable increase in costs?

Is the goal attainable with CAL? Is genuine and useful interaction possible? Can you articulate the knowledge and skills of the master performer?

How much variety will you allow the student to express? What sort of mix do you envisage between giving the student complete freedom to enter anything and severely restricting the legal choices?

Is the problem analogous to any other that would suggest a courseware solution? Can you copy, modify, or otherwise transport other courseware solutions?

What resources (money, machines, people, time) do you have that make a computer solution feasible? What constraints must you consider?

What will students see when they work through the lesson? Can you create a storyboard and/or set of sample screens for at least the start of your lesson (about three or so exchanges) that will show the general lines your lesson will take and help you to anticipate what the lesson will look like from the student's perspective?

two

TOWARD INTELLIGENT COURSEWARE

chapter **7**

Why Scripted Courseware Isn't Good Enough

IN THIS CHAPTER

■ We consider some theoretical explanations for the weakness of so much available tutorial courseware.

■ We see why scripted courseware, in which the designer anticipates a number of wrong answers and prepares instruction for them, is useful for simple learning tasks, such as assimilating or memorizing information, but for more complex kinds of learning, we need more powerful approaches.

■ We identify three major deficiencies of scripted courseware. It does not
  • let students express the full range of their variety
  • model students
  • give students a chance to talk about what they're doing

■ Once we go beyond relatively simple goals in teaching and try to emulate what really happens in a human exchange, the absence of these things becomes critical.

■ We see that, given our present knowledge about what constitutes good instruction, designing these three attributes into courseware is a difficult and only partially understood task.

WHEN JOHNNY CAN'T ADD

The following dialogue is fictional, but any resemblance to real courseware, living or dead, is purely intentional.

111

TEACHER: Johnny, how much is 2 + 2? Is it 4? or 5? or 6? or 7? or 8?
JOHNNY: It's 3.
TEACHER: I'm sorry, Johnny. "3" isn't on my list of wrong answers.
           Try again. But remember, you have to choose from the
           ones I give you.
JOHNNY: But I don't like your wrong answers. I like mine. 3.
TEACHER: Johnny, you're a bad student with a bad attitude, and I'm
           going to put that on your report card.

What would we say of a classroom teacher who would accept only some wrong answers but refused to talk about others? What should we say about courseware that accepts only some wrong answers but refuses to talk about others? Of course, "inability" is more accurate than "refusal." We can see the reasons for this inability in the basic assumptions of frame-based, scripted courseware paradigm.

The frame, as we saw in Chapter 1, is the basic organizational unit of much courseware. Its primary function is to allow the designer to control the display of, and access to, subject matter. It is a perfectly logical organizational method, but the term *frame* has also come to mean a "scripted" instructional style: The designer prepares a scenario in which the lesson asks questions and anticipates responses; the script dictates that the student be branched to various portions of the material on the basis of those responses. The constraints of both the designer's time and the computer's memory mean that only a relatively few responses can be predicted and dealt with, and this is so whether we speak of multiple-choice or constructed-response questions.

THE AMBIGUOUS RESEARCH ON COURSEWARE

Scripted courseware has its merits and its place. With fairly simple and straightforward objectives—exposing students to a body of information or practicing simple skills—branching, scripted courseware can prove effective, save time, and help weaker students. But for reaching more complex goals, we lack unequivocal evidence.[1] Edwards, Norton, Weiss, and Van Dusseldorp (1975) and Thomas (1979) are fairly positive in their assessment of scripted CAL, but Hausman (1979) is somewhat less enthusiastic, speaking more of "potential." In an early, more exhaustive review of the literature, Rockart and Morton (1975) report "ambiguous results," noting the difficulty of finding well-controlled research.

Later research like Brebner et al. (1980), Dence (1980), Hallsworth and Brebner (1980), and Gershman and Sakamoto (1980) also suggest ambiguous or inconclusive results. Sophisticated "meta-studies" by Kulik and his associates (1980, 1983, 1983a) indicate that courseware success is limited

---

[1] As with educational research generally, it's difficult to produce controlled experiments about scripted courseware since one can't truly duplicate the laboratory conditions of the physical scientist. The literature tends to report less than fully controlled studies with results that aren't conclusive.

to clearly demarcated situations like short-term studies, elementary and secondary school curricula, and lower-level cognitive objectives. Further, results show a large variability, with many students learning just as well with other media. More hostile early critics such as Oetinger and Marks (1969) and Nelson (1974), and even sympathetic ones like Kearsley (1977), point out theoretical problems that scripted courseware still has not solved, even many years after the criticisms were first made.

More distressing is that few studies show whether skills are transferred from the lessons to other parts of the curriculum. To choose a single (although frequently encountered) courseware subject: a number of lessons exist that teach writing skills by presenting the student with error-filled sentences. Regardless of how well students score on the achievement tests at the end of the lessons, their ability to transfer these skills to their own essays—when that is even measured—remains severely limited. This suggests that whatever goes on in the composition process is clearly more complex than what apparently can be taught with courseware that functions essentially as an electronic workbook, albeit a book that turns its own pages.

THE WRONG PARADIGM

Programs that teach writing skills by using prepared or "canned" sentences are very inflexible, despite claims for individualized learning. If students don't like the choices offered, the lesson can't do much for them beyond displaying, "Your answer wasn't expected—try again." Attempts to provide more flexibility by offering more choice must quickly face the persistent issue of just how much can be added, given the constraints of the designer's cleverness in anticipating possible wrong answers and the problems of storage and retrieval. As designers of scripted lessons try to become more responsive to a great many students, they confront an inevitable combinatorial explosion of things that must be programmed.[2]

It is, of course, unfair to attack courseware for what other media don't do well either. Educators, for example, decry not only that writing is generally poorly taught, they also debate *what* should be taught and how. For some, any workbook approach to writing skills—one that concentrates on grammar more than composition—does little good whether delivered in classrooms or on computers. Indeed, some teachers argue that grammar should be relegated to a distant place behind a more holistic, "creative" approach to writing. Such logic implies that we should use computers only for the truly mechanical parts of teaching writing, like word processing or spelling checks. That may well be what we ultimately decide, but students will always have to know enough grammar and usage to make themselves understood. However, the issue is not confined to what should be in the curriculum: we should also ask if the scripted workbook approach to language teaching really tests limits of educational computing. What we

---

[2] For instance, a sentence with five separate errors—not an unrealistic number for a remedial student—has 32 possible combinations of corrections.

have now may not work very well because we are designing courseware to behave like books.

SYSTEMS THINKING

A potent objection to all scripted CAL, even from the vantage point of the simplest sort of learning theory, is its implicit assumption that learning involves only discriminating among alternatives. For this must be the case in a lesson that specifies in advance the number of things from which the student can choose and to which it is prepared to respond. This restriction applies whether students pick letters or construct their own answers that must come from a small subset of all possible answers. In both cases, the lesson can deal only with a limited range of responses. The result is that scripted CAL considers only a small part of the whole learning process, ignoring some fundamental principles that have been well known to systems theorists for many years.

Why should we turn to systems theory when addressing education? Because learning is a complex interplay of students, teachers, and subject matter. Any one by itself is a highly complex entity, capable of assuming many different states of being. Each component affects the others. One kind of student will prompt one kind of teacher to perform one way while a second will evince a quite different response. One subject matter will call for one organization and approach; another again demands something quite distinct. At any given moment, learning might involve so many separate combinations of cognitive styles, subject domains, or tutoring strategies, all in various changing degrees of interplay, that a full description is virtually impossible. But there are a number of ideas we can use to begin to approach such complexity. They are not explicit design tools for courseware—we can't follow them like algorithms—but they are ways of thinking about fundamental design issues.

THE NEED TO LET THE STUDENT SHOW HIS COMPLEXITY

The first such idea, called "The Law of Requisite Variety," (Ashby 1964) tells us that in order to cope with a system's variety (that is, the number of different states it can assume), we have to have at least as much variety available to us as does that system. Metaphorically, for example, teaching becomes a game in which both players win if one (the teacher) can change the thinking and behavior of the other (the student). For every move the student makes (saying that $2 + 2$ is 3), the teacher must have a countermove, and that ought to be more than simply telling someone to choose one of the "right" wrong answers—one the computer has a ready response to.

Because students interact with subject matter, teachers, and other students, as well as their own histories, skills, and feelings, they can generate a huge variety of responses to any question courseware might put. Some answers will be right, others not. But all of them will be important: For with what else except the response can we take the measure of what is going on in a student's mind? Naturally, even the most generous-minded teachers draw a line about how freely students may answer. Seventh-grade teachers don't mind reviewing sixth-grade material, but work more appropriate to a fifth or fourth grader is another matter. Courseware is not even so generous, usually drawing its line at three possibilities. (Or four or five, but—alas— what fundamental difference does this make?) Yet any classroom teacher knows there are more than just a few wrong answers to any question.

WHICH VARIETY IS MORE INTERESTING—THE DESIGNER'S OR STUDENT'S?

Stafford Beer (1981) has argued that computers, as they are most often used, respond only to a very much "attenuated variety" of their users; worse, "It is the computer that generates the variety and not the real world. This is quite fundamental nonsense." In much courseware, the machine displays page after page of text, pictures, or questions, leaving the student little to do other than pressing a key every now and then. It is the designer's variety that increases as he tries to anticipate more and more wrong responses with more and more frames until he strikes the wall of what can be anticipated, stored, and retrieved. The true focal point of what is taking place is not, therefore, the variety of knowledge and needs the student actually possesses, his strengths and weaknesses, conceptions and misconceptions, as they should be permitted to emerge. Yet that, as anyone who has ever been in a classroom knows, must be at the dead center of instruction.

HELPING STUDENTS COMPOSE, NOT CHOOSE

Here is a more real-world example than our opening dialogue between Johnny and the machine teaching 2 + 2. Assume you're asked to design courseware to teach writing skills. Because writing is a complex act involving such difficult-to-describe skills as understanding and organizing and such even more difficult-to-describe products as style, you start with instruction on the rules of grammar and punctuation, topics about which there is a helpful consensus. Your first design could be typical of most courseware: a presentation of a rule, a display with a few examples, and an exercise with a sentence that has an error corresponding to the rule being taught. Vary the number of exercises and the number of errors in each sentence, record the number of right and wrong answers, and you are pretty much in the courseware mainstream. You have retained the basic instructional strategy of displaying a sentence and asking the student to identify or correct the error.

Yet composition means exactly that: composing, creating a whole out of diverse elements. It doesn't mean recognizing errors in somebody else's sentence, although this may indeed be a necessary prerequisite to writing error-free sentences of one's own. Again, this is as much a criticism of the curriculum as courseware. As linguists have been saying for many years, what is truly important about the way humans use language is their ability to generate (and of course understand) utterances that no one else has ever generated before. When we ask students to write, we are asking them to think about some particular topic and generate a series of sentences. What emerges is a great variety of sentences, some good, others bad, and still others somewhere in between. All sentences reflect their writers: the particular conceptions and misconceptions they have about writing and, just as revealing, the absence of certain conceptions. It is *those* sentences we must examine if we wish to guide students towards good writing.

But this is not what happens in the typical CAL lesson with its workbook approach to teaching. That great variety and novelty of student sentences—the important variety and novelty—never emerges. Instead, the focus is on the variety of the computer with its explanations, prompts, and examples. The student sits quietly by, occasionally entering a word or a letter which the program then tries to match to one of its anticipated responses. A lesson that works in these terms does so because it restricts the student to a narrowly defined subset of possible answers. But there is no necessary reason why any of these answers would reflect the process of writers struggling to learn writing. It is no wonder that learning seldom occurs.

WHEN STUDENTS CAN'T COMPOSE: THE TRANSFERENCE OF KNOWLEDGE

And lest we think "seldom" is too harsh, consider the amount of transference (the application of what one has learned to a different situation) that one is likely to see. There are very few studies that report (positively or otherwise) on how much better compositions are after students go through courseware that teaches writing. Post-test scores by themselves are not fair measures since they, too, ask students to identify errors in someone else's sentence, rather than generating new sentences. It is indeed quite hard even to find studies that try to measure transference to essays: Although what other objective should a writing lesson have?

One study that did consider transference (Merrill, Schneider, and Fletcher, 1980) looked at one of the most ambitious systems to teach language arts (as well as other subjects), the TICCIT project.[3] A thorough-going effort to teach grammatical skills by means of scripted courseware, TICCIT's lessons were augmented by excellent graphics and learner control. However, they provided for little in the way of student input beyond one-word answers. Although post-test scores showed in the high 80s, essay grades were no better than C–. Whatever else was being taught, it apparently wasn't composition. And this was true despite an exceptionally sophisticated and careful rendering of the frame-based paradigm.

[3] We'll look at TICCIT again in a different context in Chapter 10.

Another study that tried to measure such transference was Keller (1982), which reported on the development of about 12 hours of courseware that also taught grammar. Despite significant enhancement in the amount and scope of branching, an increase in the number of errors presented in each sentence, and the high grades recorded on the post tests, essay scores showed little or no improvement. Students simply were not able to take what they putatively had learned on the CAL lessons and transfer it to their own writing. Time and again, the sentences they themselves wrote showed precisely the errors they had been able to correct on the scripted lessons and posttests.

Interviews with students suggested that they looked for errors only on the lesson's sentences rather than their own because the lessons had not shown them how to compose and then revise sentences. We should note that the courseware's objective was not to have students produce well-thought-out or stylistically good essays. However, the essays still showed the very errors that post-test results say should not have been made. The conclusion of that study was that the scripted paradigm itself was to blame since by its very nature it did not address the skills needed for writing essays but only those needed to recognize errors in already existing sentences.

Again, one might well blame the curriculum that included looking for errors in canned sentences. But courseware designers also are culpable because their work tends to accept the limits of the workbook, instead of trying to go past it. In brief, the transfer of skills from either workbook or scripted lessons to essays does not take place because nowhere does the strategy come to terms with the variety of the student's strengths and weaknesses. Clearly, we don't exploit the computer by importing the design principles of the workbook.

The research doesn't merely reflect the difficulties of teaching grammar but also the limits of scripted courseware. As long as students never receive an opportunity to display what they think about the subject—good, bad, or indifferent—we simply can't infer what their problems are and then offer appropriate help. All we can do is anticipate still more wrong answers, a finally impossible and wrongheaded approach that only increases the already considerable variety of the machine, rather than the student's own variety. The solution is to find ways to extend a lesson so it accepts and responds to the complexities of what students really know.

THE NEED TO MODEL THE STUDENT'S COMPLEXITY

We not only need to let Johnny say that $2 + 2 = 3$, but we have to understand what that implies for instruction. A second systems law is the corollary of Requisite Variety: to regulate something requires a model of the thing being regulated. Good teachers always do this, of course. When students give wrong answers, good teachers attempt to reconstruct the thinking process in their own minds. Most courseware does keep some kind of records about the student: how many tries for each question, the number of right and wrong answers, perhaps the path through the various branches or time spent at the computer. But these are things that are easy to know, not necessarily important to know.[4] They don't tell us much about what we'd really like to know:

> Why do some students respond in certain ways?
> How is knowledge arranged in their minds?
> What misconceptions and gaps are present?
> How do their goals and ours mesh?
> How have our questions constrained expression of their real states of mind?
> What strategies do they use to solve problems?

To this brief list, one can easily add many more, which doesn't mean, of course, that it's easy to discover the answers. But here again is Stafford Beer (1981): "The constraint that maybe we don't know in the least what we are talking about is the most practical of them all—and the most likely." Any lesson that contents itself simply with scores, number of attempts, or even pathways through the lesson cannot build a genuinely useful model of the student it tries to teach. And without that model, it can't regulate behavior.

THE NEED TO LET THE STUDENT TALK ABOUT COMPLEXITY

A third systems notion we can use in designing courseware involves a "metalanguage" to describe what goes on at a global level when students learn. That is, in addition to the level where we note that "3" wasn't right, we also must talk with students about their plans, strategies, and goals. Both we and they have to know which plans worked or were ineffective, which ones they should call upon in which situations, which techniques to discard and which to retain. In short, we need a strategy *about* strategies so that both student and teacher can communicate on the subject of the whole learning process, stepping outside, as it were, immediate concerns such as "2 + 2." Gordon Pask, the British cybernetician and epistemologist, speaks of an executive that directs the attention of the student and allocates the resources of lower-level operations (Pask 1975). That's precisely what is needed in courseware.

Relatively few lessons even consider the need of a metalanguage. Some do have advising and help facilities, a few permit the student some control of the pace and content. But again, this isn't enough if students are going to develop overall strategies for learning that would help them introspect about what they're doing. This is not to say that we are at the point where such lessons are going to be abundant. But we have to recognize an impasse and think how to go beyond it.

[4] There are programs that report, for instance, response time down to milliseconds. One wonders why.

Again, let's briefly look at teaching writing skills as a concrete example. In a hypothetical student sentence, the possible causes for error include not knowing the constituent parts of the sentence nor the rules for manipulating them, but also not knowing how to organize whatever knowledge the writer does, in fact, have. It isn't enough for students to think about just one sentence, however; they have to be able to think about any they might write. They have to step back and be able to talk to themselves as well as to their teachers about sentences in general. So courseware that truly simulates a human tutor must get the student to ask questions like "Is this a noun clause?", "What rules apply to what I've written?", or "Where's the best place to begin?" And it should support the answering of them too.

The questions students ask themselves will vary according to the subject matter and to the tutoring style. The timing and the frequency of these questions also require some kind of overview (if not a theory of instruction) about how much help to offer and when. Despite these obstacles, we have to remember the weakness of most courseware: When we give only a right answer, all that has been learned is that one answer. But when we give a strategy for finding answers, we've taught something worthy.

SIMULATIONS AND INTELLIGENT CAL: TOWARD BETTER PARADIGMS

Most available courseware doesn't permit variety, model students, or let learners talk about what they're doing. To some degree, that can be traced to limits of the curriculum that imposes workbook exercises. In terms of the medium itself, however, once we go beyond the relatively simple goals in teaching and try to emulate what really happens in a human exchange, the absence of the necessary attributes of good courseware becomes critical. The limits of the curriculum are one constraint designers face, but perhaps not the deciding one. Rather than simply copying techniques of the workbook, we should set out to use the computer in ways not possible with a workbook. We need better paradigms.

One possibility lies in greater use of simulations. The chapter that follows examines some of the principles behind their design. Perhaps even a better paradigm lies in work that has been going on since the 1970s under the rubric of Intelligent Computer-Assisted Instruction. ICAI owes much to work in Artificial Intelligence, whose researchers have explored many of the issues of learning and teaching. ICAI work offers us no easy path to follow or code to copy, pseudo or otherwise. Moreover, the most interesting ICAI requires computing power still beyond most current hardware. Yet there are some techniques we can use now, and the rest of this book is about them. The chapters that follow, however, are not detailed *how-to* guides as much as they are explorations of what general principles underlie the design of simulations and intelligent courseware.

SUMMARY

Scripted courseware, in which the designer prepares material for a number of anticipated wrong answers, can be used for simple learning tasks, but it does not afford students a wide range of responses, responses that reflect the variety and novelty of which learners are capable. Nor does it construct a useful model of the individual student. Finally, it cannot provide students with a metalanguage for their learning activity. Simulation and Intelligent Computer-Assisted Instruction (ICAI), which are explored in the remainder of this book, suggest techniques we can follow now to remedy these three deficiencies.

REFERENCES

Ashby, W. R. *An Introduction To Cybernetics* (London: Methuen, 1964).
Beer, S. *Platform for Change* (London: Wiley, 1975).
———*Death is Equifinal* (unpublished address to the Society for General Systems Research, Toronto, 1981). Brebner, A., Hallsworth, H. J., McIntosh, E. and Wonter, C. J. "Teaching Elementary Reading by CMI and CAI," *Association for Educational Data Systems: Convention Proceedings* (1980).
Dence, M. "Toward Defining A Role for CAI: A Review," *Educational Technology,* 20 (11) (1980), 50–54.
Edwards, J., Norton S., Weiss, M., and Van Dusseldorp, R. "How Effective Is CAI? A Review of Research," *Educational Leadership, 33,* 147–53.
Gershman, J. and Sakamota, E. "Computer-Assisted Remediation and Evaluation: A CAI Project for Ontario Secondary Schools," *Educational Technology,* 21(3) (1980), 40–43.
Hausmann, K. (1979) Instructional Computing in Higher Education. *AEDS Monitor,* 18 (4,5,6), 32–37.
Hallsworth, H. J. and Brebner, A. *Computer-Assisted Instruction in Schools: Achievements, Present Developments and Projections for the Future.* (Calgary: Faculty of Education, Computer Applications Unit, 1980).
Kearsley, G. P. "Some Conceptual Issues in Computer-Assisted Instruction," *Journal of Computer-Based Instruction,* 4 (1) (1977), 8–16.
Keller, A. *The Comma Converser: An Intelligent CAL Program to Teach the Use of the Comma* (unpublished Ph.D. dissertation, Concordia University, Montreal, 1982).
Kulik, J. A., Kulik, C.–L. C, and Cohen P. "Effectiveness of Computer-Based College Teaching: A Meta-Analysis of Finding." *Review of Educational Research,* 50(4) (1980), 525–44.
Kulik, J. A. and Bangert-Drowns, R. L. "Effectiveness of Technology in Precollege Mathematics and Science Teaching," *Journal of Educational Systems,* 12(2) (1983), 137–59.
Kulik, J. A., Bangert, R. L., and Williams, G. W. "Effects of Computer-Based Teaching on Secondary School Students," *Journal of Educational Psychology,* 75(1) (1983a), 19–26.
Merrill, H. D. Schneider, E. Fletcher, K. *TICCIT.* (Englewood Cliffs, N. J.: Educational Technology Publications, 1980).
Nelson, T. N. *Computer Lib* (Chicago, 1974).

Oettinger, A. G. and Marks, S. *Run, Computer, Run: The Mythology of Educational Innovation* (Cambridge, Mass: Harvard University Press. 1969).

Pask, G. *Conversation, Cognition, and Learning* (Amsterdam and New York: Elsevier, 1975).

Rockart, J. F. and Morton, M. S. *Computers and the Learning Process in Higher Education* (New York: McGraw-Hill, 1975).

Thomas, D. B. (1979) "The effectiveness of Computer-assisted instruction in secondary schools," *AEDS Monitor,* 12(3), 103–116.

chapter 8

Simulations: The Next Best Things

IN THIS CHAPTER

- We examine the basic architecture of CAL simulations—scaled-down enactments of complex realities.
- We recognize simulations as being quite different from tutorial courseware both in spirit and in form: less concerned with students' achieving specific results and more concerned with student exploration.
- In contexts where performing the necessary work is either time-consuming, dangerous, or expensive, we find simulations permitting students to manipulate models of the world in question.
- Three major problems in designing simulations are identified:
    - developing models of reality;
    - coping with the necessary complicated programming;
    - situating simulations within a curriculum.
- The most successful simulations are found to be those which draw upon reasonably clear systems (like customers being served in a bank or a set of players in a card game), because key components are readily seen and relationships can be expressed.
- We divide simple simulations into three major parts:
    1. an *environment,* which is a world analogous to some other world that is of real interest
    2. *players* who move in that world, taking any of a set of actions that the designer declares "legal"
    3. *outcomes,* which specify the effect of those moves on both environment and players

SAVING SWIMMERS: WHY TO USE SIMULATIONS AND WHERE

Assume these are prehistoric times and you a Neanderthal swimming instructor. You probably teach your craft by grasping students firmly at both ends and tossing them smartly into the water. If the waters are shark-infested, well, so much greater their desire to learn. Whatever the merits of such teaching (lessons don't take much time, grading is simple, unsuccessful learners can't complain), the "sink or swim or be eaten" approach in so drastic a form isn't much recommended in these enlightened days. A post-Neanderthal swimming instructor can either take the more kindly Red Cross approach or else turn to a simulation with make-believe nonswimmers and make-believe sharks.

THE MAJOR ADVANTAGES

A simulation is an imitation of some portion of reality, designed to capture its essential elements while avoiding its hazards and inconveniences. In a good simulation, the user interacts with an environment that is analogous to another (the real and more interesting one) and so vicariously experiences it.

Safety and Convenience There are many times when we would like users to examine and explore a system without actually coming into direct contact with it. Consider the obvious training problems of the nuclear industry: There are no small mistakes. Consider the problems of teaching genetics: even fruit flies take weeks to show interesting mutations. A nuclear simulator can remove the risks of instructing novices; a genetic simulator can end protracted waits for mating and mutating fruit flies.

Motivation In addition to safety and convenience, a good simulation motivates because, like a good teacher, it inspires. Nothing else—except for a direct contact with the reality in question—allows students to enter into and explore a world so well. As students move through a simulated world, changing its environment, they quickly see the results of what they've done. For example:

A valve in a steam engine is opened; the internal heat increases.

The flaps of an aircraft simulator move; the plane descends.

The average temperature of a continent increases by two degrees; some regions bloom, some become desert.

The computer's capacity to keep track of complexity and to provide students with an immediate response makes it an ideal medium for designing and presenting simulations.

LEARNING THROUGH WORLDS TO EXPLORE

Simulations imply a very much different notion of the instructional uses of computers than courseware tutorials or drill and practice programs. A simulation doesn't so much direct students towards very explicit ends as much as it encourages them to discover what is implicit. We can think about simulations a little as we think about LOGO—as a world to explore.

LOGO is far more than just another programming language; it is a world where a triangular-shaped turtle traces patterns as it moves. To control events in that world (to make the triangle trace the outline of a square, for instance) requires the user to master specific skills, not as ends in themselves but as a means to solving various problems such as tracing a square. A child may explicitly learn the concepts of going forward and turning right or left, but the particular ends to which that knowledge is put are not specified by LOGO. Some children will successfully produce squares, some other children will just as successfully produce something else. LOGO's appeal lies in its granting the freedom to explore a world and ask "what if"? what if Turtle turns right 91 degrees instead of 90? A tutorial in geometry might tell us directly; LOGO lets us discover the implications of our choices.

The same is true for a simulation. Students explore an environment, setting events in motion and watching the results. Simulations don't emphasize mastery of specific skills or knowledge as courseware does. Instead, they stress discovering, asking "what if" questions and having the computer answer by carrying out the necessary actions. Students acquire requisite skills and knowledge indirectly in the course of their explorations. Neither does the designer of a simulation try to anticipate everything a student might ask and supply a specific answer. Like the designers of LOGO, designers of simulations try to create the worlds in which students can bring about demonstrations of the relationships among elements in a given environment.

SOME SUCCESSFUL EXAMPLES

Many kinds of simulations have been designed. We've already mentioned nuclear reactors and the mutating genes of fruit flies. Another well-known example is found in operational research, where a frequently taught topic is the queuing problem that determines how long it takes someone in a line to be served. Think of your bank on a busy day: How many more tellers would it take to reduce your wait? There are mathematical formulas that allow one to compute this, but they are useful really only when the numbers of customers and tellers are fairly small. In large and complicated systems, the only feasible way to discover how long the wait will be is to run a simulation where customers arrive in the queue by some previously observed frequency, are served according to a known average serving time, and leave to be replaced by new customers. A simulation allows students to observe the lines lengthening and shortening from those that are irritatingly long to those with no one in them at all—and in only a fraction of the effort and time involved in borrowing a bank for a day. Moreover, by allowing students to change key variables (number of arrivals in a given time, average time to serve a customer, etc.), we help them develop a sense of the real-world tradeoffs between the costs of hiring more tellers and the costs of losing disgruntled customers.

Similarly, programs for medical students exist that present symptoms of hypothetical patients. The novice doctors extend their diagnostic and treatment skills, deciding what disease a particular combination of symptoms and history points to and what treatment they should prescribe. This can be done many times over, with a great variety of patients, in far less time than an actual clinic would need and without endangering anyone.

The list of possible examples continues:

We might train students in urban studies with a simulation that draws on a data base of facts about a city's resources. This information then could be used in simulated exchanges between opposing interest groups. The student could see how the scarce resources of a city government might be allocated between competing claims (say, a community center or more police protection).

Architectural students can design structures and submit them to simulated hurricanes.

Military strategists can refight major battles, changing original tactics and weaponry and seeing new outcomes.

And, perhaps most effectively, natural sciences simulations can place students in virtually every sort of laboratory.

The sample lesson on the fulcrum in Chapter 3 was in fact a physics simulation of the laws of levers. Other examples (among many, many) have been in the flow of electrons in crystals, the competition among animals for food in an ecological chain, and experiments in radiation. (See Tawney 1979.)

DESIGNING SIMULATIONS: THREE MAJOR PROBLEMS

There are three problems in designing simulations:

1. modeling reality
2. coding the simulation
3. situating the simulation within the curriculum

Modeling reality   What makes possible all of these simulations is that their designers have been able to abstract the essential elements and interrelationships of some real experience. Designers have, in other words, modeled something. The components of that model can then be manipulated by an agent (the student or the computer) according to a set of well-defined rules. The rules that describe interactions among system components determine what happens. Like the generative courseware programs we saw in Chapter 3, simulation programs require that whatever data is used be manipulated in predictable ways. The equivalent to the master performer's equation that $A + B = C$ is a model of a system, its set of rules, that operate just as consistently as A and B always adding up to C.

The obvious difficulty is to create that model initially, to put in place a master performer's knowledge about the system of interest. In some instances, as in the fulcrum problem, the model *is* an equation (or a group of them) that is readily programmable and which indeed does capture what is central to the system. With other simulations, such as ones to teach genetics or queuing theory, enough of a mathematical foundation exists for us to state a reasonable portion of the system's main features. But in other complex cases—in urban studies or in military planning, for example—the model is far less clear.

Expert knowledge is crucial in any teaching program but especially in simulations. In a tutorial, missing facts are simply that—missing. But in a simulation, missing items can result in a model so simple as to no longer usefully reflect reality. Presenting such partial knowledge to the student means presenting a misleading picture because the real world won't be much like the simulated one. Worse: if the simulation happens to be of something dangerous—like airplane flying—the experience goes from merely useless to resolutely hazardous the day students try out what they think they've learned.

The complications of programming   Even with a model that captures the essential flavor of some system, we still face considerable and complicated programming. Special simulation languages help keep up with the vast number of variables of a complex system, but it's not easy going. Any interesting system, after all, will have more complexity than a human can think of all at once—or why else use a computer?

Where in the curriculum?   And there is a third problem, specific to CAL. If its primary intention is to teach, a simulation must be clearly situated within a curriculum. Unlike a tutorial, which can operate as a stand-alone program, or even a drill-and-practice lesson, which can be used with relatively small amounts of prior instruction, a simulation must assume the student has basic knowledge of the world on which it draws. Both student and classroom teacher must know where the simulation fits into the rest of the curriculum. There is not much point in giving students a system, letting them vary inputs and watch outputs, if they haven't much notion of what is really going on. So in addition to the problems of creating a model, executing it in terms of computer code, and producing the necessary bookkeeping and management facilities, the designer has both to articulate a simulation's role in instruction and prepare (or at least provide access to) other materials. For that, a detailed instructional design is necessary.

It follows, then, that we can't design simulations unless we have a fair amount of knowledge, energy, and experience. This single chapter can't show the details of how to create the model of anything of great complexity, far less how to put it into a simulation. Moreover, there's no guarantee that it would be about a topic that interests you. However, a chapter can show something of the basic architecture of a simulation, and with that in hand, you can begin to think of designing your own.

THE THREE BASIC COMPONENTS OF SIMULATION

A simulation requires you to design three basic things:

1. an *environment*
2. a set of *players* who can take certain agreed-upon actions within that environment
3. a set of *rules* that specify the results those actions will have on both the environment and the players themselves

The environment By environment, we mean a world, analogous to some other, whose set of identifiable features and their interrelationships can be stated without ambiguity. In physics, for instance, we might be interested in fulcrums and how they behave; in a simulation, the fulcrum becomes a picture of a seesaw and two weights. In urban studies, we might wish to know about people who live in big cities; for a simulation, we would construct a data base holding facts about a population with regard to income, race, education, voting patterns, and so on. For a program to teach medical diagnoses, we would build another sort of data base—one about patients, their symptoms, their histories, and their treatment.

The players When we speak of players, we mean a group of well-defined entities who, operating under the set of constraints the simulation imposes, make specified legal moves. Players can be human (like customers in a bank) or nonhuman (like natural objects or forces). A player's move is legal because it makes the simulation possible; a legal move can be quite distinct from a move which a player might take in the real world. For instance, a legal move for a player in the fulcrum simulation could be placing a block anywhere on one side of the seesaw; an illegal move would be placing two on the same side. Nothing in the laws of physics says that two weights can't be on the same side, but a simulation needs a constraint like this rule if it's going to work.

Similarly, a player's legal move might be to choose only blocks weighing between 100 and 500 pounds. The rules of a fulcrum would still apply if the weights fell outside this range, but the demonstration's effectiveness would be compromised. For the patient simulation, legal moves might include the novice doctor asking about symptoms, requesting tests, or administering particular drugs. Illegal moves might be asking about political affiliations, religious beliefs, or income. In some cases, therefore, we define what is legal because we want to make the simulation genuinely approximate reality; in others, we want to impose a constraint to make sure the simulation's teaching works.

The rules   Finally, by "rules that specify outcomes" we mean a set of statements that articulates what happens as a result of a player's legal move. In the fulcrum simulation, placing a 100-pound weight twice as far from the fulcrum as a 200-pound weight on the other side results in a balanced seesaw. A novice doctor's legal move in diagnosing and prescribing may either cure or kill the patient. A social planner's decision to spend money on a recreation center instead of more police may produce less crime. And so on. In summary, there must be

> a world,
> players who move within it, and
> a well-defined set of consequences for those moves

GAMES AND SIMULATIONS

Games and simulations have several features in common. Both require environments, players, and ways of determining outcomes. Both range from the very simple (tic-tac-toe and the fulcrum) to the very complex (chess and the behavior of patients). Much of what follows about constructing simulations can be applied to games. The essential difference is that games are inherently competitive whether the opponent is another human or (as often happens) a computer program.[1] In an educational game, students win to the degree they master skills. Learning, if not altogether play, becomes fun as students get swept up through the challenge of competition. In a simulation, however, the issue isn't winning or losing but rather inquiring about some complex system.

In simulations, the student recognizes much more explicitly than in a game that the end is learning, and that fun is a pleasant bonus. This added dimension of pleasure while learning certainly has been a major reason for the popularity of both games and simulations, indeed sometimes at the expense of anything else. Without sounding needlessly cranky, we should remind ourselves that fun does not guarantee effective learning, any more than does drudgery. Like all other learning activities, games and simulations must finally be judged by how much the student learns. The instructional-design schemes in Chapter 1 must be as much in evidence for designing games and simulations as for tutorial courseware.

---

[1] There are also cooperative games where the object is not winning as much as learning how to work with others.

A STRAIGHTFORWARD EXAMPLE: DRAW POKER

To show the general procedures for designing simulations, we will begin with the game of poker. Although persons without much experience in playing the game might think its outcome is based on chance, poker is an interesting game both of probability and psychology. As such it provides, in addition to its own intrinsic interest, an environment to show students how the laws of probability work. It also can allow students to look at the consequences of human decisions in the face of both those laws and the decisions of others.

We'll use the game of poker here not to pit one player against another but to simulate probability and human psychology. The poker variant we'll use is draw poker, a game in which five cards are dealt to a player who then has the right to discard up to four of them and "draw" replacements. The object of the game is to get the highest-ranking hand among those players still actively betting at the end. There are two rounds of betting: once, after the first five cards have been dealt, and again, after the draw has taken place.

Building the Environment

The first problem is to build a computer world analogous to a real one in which cards are dealt and bets made. Assuming there will be five players,[2] we will need to be ready to deal 45 cards: 25 in the first round, plus another 20 in case all five players want their full complement of four new cards. There is no need to ready 52 cards, since the last seven will never be drawn, and selecting these last cards can be time-consuming.

Getting the Cards on the Table

To prepare the environment, we create a list of all the cards in the deck, assigning each one a unique number between 1 and 52. That is, we might arbitrarily have 1 as the ace of spades, 2 as the 2 of spades, and so on. This done, we generate 45 different random numbers from 1 to 52, giving every card in the full deck an equal chance of being picked. Note this is not the same as generating a random number between 1 and 52 45 times, since in that instance, we'd be sure to get duplicates.

With 45 numbers matching 45 cards, we then distribute five cards to each player. If the first five numbers are, suppose, 19, 26, 44, 1, 9, and the numbers stand for, again suppose, the queen of hearts, jack of diamonds, etc., these cards would constitute Player #1's hand before the draw. We repeat this for Player #2 and for all subsequent players until the first 25 cards have been distributed. Obviously, we must also record somewhere who has what. Even in these preliminaries, the bookkeeping gets involved—which is why we need our computer.

---

[2] Poker works best with five players, but one could have as few as two or as many as seven.

When all five players' hands have been recorded, we need to rank them against each other. This allows us to decide how much each hand will bet, perhaps as a percentage of the player's current winnings. Everyone starts off with equal stakes, players being declared out of the game when their money falls below a certain amount or when they are bankrupt. The winner will be either the only player with any money or the one with the most after a given number of hands.

The next part of the game requires us to remove the deadwood (that is, what players wish to discard) from the list containing each player's hand and to replace them via the draw. Which cards actually get discarded can be the subject of the legal moves we'll discuss shortly. Players also have the right to "fold"—that is, withdraw from the action—losing only what they have already bet. Having discarded deadwood, we now use the extra, undrawn cards from the original set of 45. There may be some leftovers, but we ignore them since each new hand requires a new set of cards. The draw made, the hands are then reanalyzed, another round of betting takes place, the hands are ranked, and a winner declared.

Specifying the Players and Their Legal Moves

To this point, we have created the environment, the first of three steps in designing simulations. We now have to specify legal moves for the players. A legal move can include, in addition to those that don't violate the rules of poker itself, moves that are strategically very good or very bad. A good move, for instance, is one that takes into account the laws of probability. To give a concrete example: The probability of being dealt four of a kind is about one in 4,165 hands; the probability of being dealt exactly one pair is one in 2.37 hands. So a good move for a player being dealt one pair would be to discard three cards and bet conservatively since the odds are good that least one of his opponents has done as well or better. A very good move would be for someone with a high card of less than 10 to fold quickly. A very poor move would be to keep all five cards in such a hand and bet them heavily. Such a player is going to lose money and lose it quickly. The next task, then, is to determine the legal moves in terms of betting patterns for each player.

Determining Betting Patterns

One way we could establish betting patterns would be to adhere strictly to the laws of probability. That is, we could permit players to bet exactly that portion of their stakes which corresponds to the probability of their winning. Someone holding a straight flush, four of a kind, or full house could bet almost everything they have. Someone holding only a single ace as their high card could bet the absolute minimum or quit. (The probabilities for each betting pattern can be obtained from the many texts on poker.) The user of the simulation can now observe the outcome of mathematical certainties and, theoretically, should see all players win as much as they lose in the long run. The decision rules here are very straightforward and automatic; the computer's role is really that of a traffic manager and scorekeeper.

But suppose rather than simulating the laws of probability, we wished to see how certain personalities might behave in certain situations. Poker, with its betting and bluffing, makes a nice laboratory for this. We could say that a legal move for Player #1 is always a reckless one; if he holds a pair, he bets 25% of his stake; if he holds two pairs, he bets 50%. (If he holds three pairs, he's recklessly dishonest.) Player #2 might be reckless too, bluffing every second hand, regardless of its strength. Player #3 might be extremely cautious, betting less than the odds indicate. Someone else could always bumble along, trying to draw a card to complete a hand despite the odds against it. These legal moves could be extended in many ways: Player #1, for instance, might increase his bet if Player #2 makes a very small one. A conservative player might simply fold if someone else makes a sizable bet. A steady loser might imprudently raise all bets. So might a steady winner. And so forth, depending on how well we ourselves can describe poker behavior.

The interest in this particular simulation now becomes the outcomes caused by different personalities reacting to similar situations. Indeed, one could construct the legal moves for a large set of players, letting the user select different combinations of them for a series of hands; the outcome would show which personality type performs best or worst against which others. The simulation could become, then, a laboratory for testing hypotheses about some kind of interaction among people, rather than just about the mathematics of poker.

Specifying Outcomes

We now need a facility to rank the hands our players hold. For this, we'll need an algorithm to arrange five cards in possible poker hands.[3] The best hand in poker is the straight flush, where a player has five cards of the same suit in order. (If the high card is the ace, this is a royal flush; you can live to be a very old poker player without ever seeing one dealt.) Here is a list of the others:

> four-of-a-kind (aces, kings, queens, etc.)
> full house (three of a kind plus a pair)
> flush (five cards of the same suit)
> straight (five cards in order, any suits)
> three of a kind
> two pairs
> one pair
> high card (that is, the value of the hand is the value of the highest card held)

[3] Levy (1983) provides comprehensive instructions about how this may be done.

The ranking facility must examine each set of five cards, see if there are duplications in rank or suit and if these duplications are potentially meaningful. For instance, four aces and a king would be a powerful hand, but four diamonds and a club would be worthless. The actual programming aside, we need a sorting program (to rank cards from high to low), a matching program capable of handling up to five duplications (of rank or suit), and a way of temporarily storing this information.[4] The ranking facility not only records what player holds what cards but also declares the winner.

A Brief Recapitulation

Let's review what we've done:

> Our poker simulation begins with an environment that is analogous to one in which five persons play.
>
> Cards are dealt, hands analyzed and ranked, bets made, a draw held, hands reanalyzed and reranked, bets made again, and a winner declared.
>
> Into this world, we can introduce a set of players who have legal moves. Such moves do not merely conform to the rules of poker but also to the laws of probability or to decisions made by specific personalities.
>
> Play continues until a set number of hands has been dealt (or time limit reached) and we determine a final winner.

Recording outcomes, the third component of a simulation, is a relatively straightforward matter here of declaring winners, both for individual rounds and over the whole session. Because players get richer or poorer, we can readily see what will happen. In other sorts of simulations, however, it is not only legal moves that are difficult to describe. Their consequences may be equally difficult to understand. Let's look at one such case.

A MESSY EXAMPLE: SIMULATING STUDENT BEHAVIOR IN A MODULAR COURSE

Let us imagine that, as an exercise, a graduate course in educational planning requires its students to redesign hypothetical introductory undergraduate courses away from traditional lectures to self-instructional modules. Instead of going to classes at specific times or doing labs and writing exams along with everyone else, students in these redesigned courses could select materials (in books, on computers, on video tape) and work through them at their own pace. If they get into in trouble, graduate students hired as tutors could see them. The exercise assumes that the materials have

---

[4] Important too is the ability to see which cards do not fall into any potential pattern at all; these cards will be the ones discarded before the draw.

already been written, money budgeted for tutors, rooms booked, and 500 students enrolled. The problem facing the would-be planners is to see if such a scheme is as workable in practice as it is in theory. Can everyone who needs or wants a specific module get it without an unacceptable delay? Will all whose cooperation is needed (tutors and students) do their parts? Will there be enough physical space for students to work in? Or will the whole program collapse under its own weight?

A way of answering these questions might simply be to run the course for a semester and see what happens. But this clearly is not possible since no ethical institution would permit such experimenting with real people. But a computer simulation would allow the student planners to see what would be happening on the fifth week, for instance, or on the tenth. The answers the simulation provides would show course designers potential pitfalls (although not necessarily how to avoid them). But what should we do, as designers of the simulation that will instruct novice planners? We start by modeling a typical set of circumstances. That is, from the mass of possibilities, we choose the salient features of 500 students going through a modularized course.

Modeling a Human System

The first part of this modeling procedure is conceptually simple. We know that we have so many students, and we know we have so many study carrels, computer facilities, tape machines, so many available hours for tutoring and lab demonstrations, and so many monitors to oversee exams. We can construct a flowchart as in Figure 8.1 that could give us an idealized view of students moving through the course.

But life is rarely so orderly. It's unlikely that such a smooth flow of students will materialize. For example, since modular courses are predicated on student choice, we must first make some guesses about which modules students are likely to choose—and not just at the beginning, but later on too. At the start of the course, and perhaps for even several weeks, the introductory lessons will be in greatest demand. However, some students will have higher entry skills and will be able to reach more advanced material more quickly. We can, therefore, predict that we'll need to provide most of the introductory lessons early on. Provided that they exist on computer or tape and that we have enough facilities for both, this won't be especially tricky. But suppose more students than we anticipate want to meet with tutors; scheduling then becomes a problem. We could arrange to spend more of our resources (the number of tutoring hours in our budget) in the first weeks to handle this rush. But we obviously leave ourselves vulnerable later.

What other factors should we include in our model? It is reasonable that the pattern of student choices will be relatively homogeneous, but we don't know that absolutely. Consider students who can choose between three or four topics. Why will they choose one over the others? Remember,

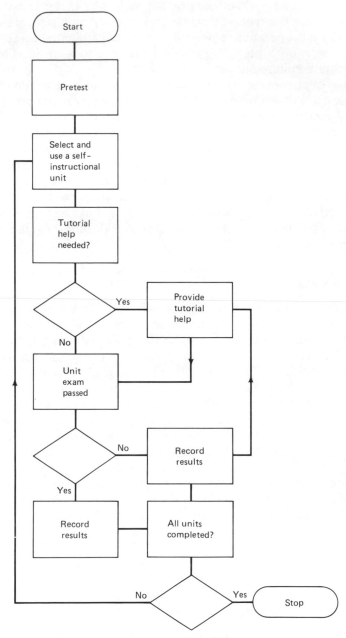

8.1 Student Path Through a Modularized Course

there is not necessarily a constraint on choice—they need not do Section 5 right after Section 4. We could assume that the choices will result from some interaction of abilities, motivation, and counseling they receive. Let's look at some of these things more closely.

Persons with a background in, say, Topic X, will probably choose Topic Y if it seems to be a natural extension of Topic X, especially when the other topics are relatively unknown to them. So we need a way of finding out what students are likely to know when they begin the course. Moreover, that entry level will have an effect later in the semester since the lessons learned at the outset will determine what will follow. Students with strong skills in one area may well try as much as they can there before going on. However, choice may not only be affected by what a student knows, but by motivation. Suppose I consider myself hopeless at math; I may well put that part of the course off until as late as possible. On the other hand, success in a topic not previously mastered may lead me to try another, similar one. The model must either assume something about the backgrounds of the students or else be prepared to find out.

Related to degree of motivation may also be the degree of counseling students get. Tutors and other students may influence choice. Everyone knows how the grapevine in a school identifies the "easy" and "interesting" courses and the effect that has on registration. However, given a well-prepared and academically ambitious student body, it may well be the challenging courses that are in the heaviest demand.

The Dilemma of Modeling Human Complexities: How Dead the End?

The modularized course model points to the essential difficulty of dealing with the kind of complexity human systems generate. We have not even considered, for example, the sheer power of human lassitude that may cause many students to ignore the course entirely until the last few weeks of the semester, instead of dutifully working throughout. So here is our dilemma: In order to produce a simulation that is genuinely useful, we must capture the main features of a system. But those features can be difficult to locate. Even assuming, for instance, that we are prepared to adjust resources to accommodate the students who leave their work until the last minute, how are we going to identify them in advance?

We could make the necessary assumptions, of course, on the basis of our experience, if we have any. Or we could use purely arbitrary numbers. In that case, even if the actual numbers were wrong, the simulation might still be a useful exercise in seeing how changing values affect the movement through the system. But this training only pushes the original problem one layer back: Given real-world demands on the course designers we wish to train, how do we proceed? The danger exists that we don't perceive patterns in the world but impose them.

WHEN SIMULATIONS DO WORK: WHAT THEY DON'T WORK AT

Even when we can design a simulation, there are still caveats when it comes to using them to teach:

A simulation is not reality   There are many simulations for laboratory work that let the student perform experiments without actually going into a lab. However, a large part of a scientist's work *is* in a laboratory; one "does science" amidst various distractions of the real lab and the recalcitrance of real data. How one learns this is a key element of the science curriculum. So however valuable a simulation may be in showing the relationship between data and theory, it can never be a substitute for the more messy world that a scientist actually will find.

And so too for our other examples. Students of urban affairs will not find groups with neatly thought-out and coherent positions. Indeed, much of their real training will consist of coaxing out positions that are resolutely incoherent. Similarly, the budding psychologist interested in how and why people take gambling decisions will not find the kind of clear rationale for actions or even the consistency the poker program implies. The medical intern, whose job often takes place in an atmosphere of crisis, will not have the relative luxury of textbook patients in the relative calm of a classroom simulation. This is not to say that the simulation will not be useful: It is to insist that a simulation is not the real thing and should not be confused for it.

Simulations don't teach the actual process of model-building Simulations don't teach the way one abstracts the key components of a system and states their relationships. Instead, simulations teach the uses to which already existing models are put. In the case of the scientist in the lab or the urban planner on the street, the truly important activity *is* creating a model, whether it be of DNA or community interaction. When we ourselves attempt to write simulations, we confront the difficulties of grasping the essential elements of a situation and recognizing their relationships. To the degree we succeed, the simulation will. But our students, changing only the inputs to a kind of blackbox and seeing only the outputs, will be doing something quite different. They aren't going to be able to model an entirely new situation for themselves. At best, they will work through the implications of our model or theory. We have, therefore, to distinguish between model-manipulating and the more important skill of model-building.

A program that tries to teach modeling may do so by having students put together parts of models that have already been chosen. As in language training, using "canned" models really teaches only discrimination among alternatives. The working scientist, however, is seldom given the simple task of choosing among preselected options. Like writers composing their own sentences, social or natural scientists generate their own possibilities and hypotheses. As valuable as simulated model building might be at relatively early stages of training, it is not a substitute for learning how to compose.

All these warnings are really not meant to dissuade one from writing simulations, although that may be the dominant impression. Still, simulations are so potentially powerful that they must be approached with caution. A badly done simulation, to repeat, is worse than useless, since it represents itself as a faithful image of reality. Someone extrapolating from it may, at best, fail in the world or, at worst, do genuine damage. The good news is that few experiences succeed as well as a good simulation because simulations offer opportunities for exploration not otherwise feasible or even possible. Simulations are not the work of a casual afternoon at the terminal. But few computer activities teach or inspire so well.

SUMMARY

Simulations consist of an environment (a world analogous to the one that is of real interest), a set of players (who exercise "legal" moves in that world), and a set of outcomes (the effects of those moves on players and environment). Simulations are best used in contexts where performing the necessary work would be either time consuming, dangerous, or expensive. They permit students to manipulate models of those realities conveniently, and the most successful of them have been those in which the designer could draw upon a system whose key components are readily seen and whose relationships are expressible mathematically.

The major problem in using simulations is that success depends on how well the designer has captured the essential details of the system to be explored. A poor model may be misleading and so be worse than useless. Two other problems are the complexities in programming and the need to situate simulations within a curriculum. Students may also confuse the simulation with the reality being modeled. Further, they practice only model-manipulation rather than model-creation.

REFERENCES

Levy, D. *Computer Gamesmanship* (New York: Simon & Schuster, 1983).
Tawney, D. A, ed. *Learning Through Computers* (London: Macmillan, 1979).

chapter 9

Coping with Student Variety: Constructing Master Performers

IN THIS CHAPTER

■ We are introduced to the *algorithm* and the *heuristic*. The first is a step-by-step, problem-solving process that always produces a correct result; the second is a general problem-solving strategy that brings us close to a correct answer but cannot guarantee one. We will look at both algorithms and heuristics so that we can design master performers into courseware.

■ We consider three principal reasons to develop master-performer algorithms and heuristics:

1. To solve the same problems we ask the student to solve. The answer produced becomes the standard against which we compare student answers. Whatever discrepancies emerge between student and master solutions allow us to make the necessary inferences about what instruction should follow.
2. To examine the student's answer, looking not for a single attribute, but for clusters of attributes in various combinations.
3. To build intelligent courseware and support systems that help students find answers.

■ There are two broad categories of algorithms and heuristics:

1. *Procedural,* which answer the question "What do I do now?"
2. *Analytic* which answer the question "What are the attributes of X?," X being a perfect or at least typical example of an object in which we are interested.

WHY WE NEED A MASTER PERFORMER'S INTELLIGENCE

The instructional design model for CAL in Chapter 1 required the following things be present:

a goal in the form of a problem the student is to solve

a master performer capable of solving that problem

a model of the student's skills as compared to the master's

a controller to choose what skills the student lacks and so decide which ones should be taught

a tutor to present material and permit the student to practice it

facilities to test the student, diagnose the causes of errors, and update the student model

Scripted CAL can have these features only in highly limited ways. If we wish to design more intelligent lessons, we have to respond to more variety from the student than single-letter or single-word answers. Students should be able to express their understanding (or lack of it) as fully as possible, just as they would with a human tutor. But if we invite variety, we must have sufficient variety of our own to cope. When students express the full range of what they think about a topic, we must have the means to see how that compares to what an expert thinks. Only then can we infer what instruction we should offer next. We therefore must first construct such experts, and in this chapter, we look at some examples and general techniques for doing so.

WHAT A MASTER PERFORMER DOES IN A LESSON

Responding to a student who can answer more fully than just a one-letter or one-word answer implies two things about a piece of courseware:

1. it can solve a problem given to the student
2. it can look at a stream of input and decide what it means and how it represents a student's attempt to solve the problem we've posed

In intelligent courseware, a master performer creates an ideal solution (or at least a "nearly perfect" one) to the problem we want the student to solve; the student's answer then is compared to the ideal one. We use the same knowledge needed to construct the master performer, moreover, to examine the student's answer.

A CONVERSATION ABOUT FRACTIONS

Later on in this chapter, we'll examine an algorithm of a master performer to add fractions. A computer program that could do this, when combined with a model of the student, can be the basis of a conversation between lesson and student about adding fractions. An example of such a conversation follows, with parenthetical comments about how the courseware is operating:

LESSON: How much is ⅓ + ⅜?
STUDENT: 4/11.
[The lesson has already solved the problem, and has compared its answer with the student's. The student error causes the lesson to take the student through the whole subtraction process.]

LESSON: No, sorry. When the numbers on the bottom of two fractions are different, we have to make them the same before we add them.
Let's go through the problem step by step.
Are the denominators—the numbers on the bottom—equal?
[This is the first step in an algorithm to add fractions.]
STUDENT: No.
[A student who would get this wrong obviously needs more help than this particular lesson has been designed to give. A wrong answer would cause the lesson to advise the student to seek different help.]

LESSON: Does 3 go into 8 without anything left over?
STUDENT: No.
[The question is based on the algorithm's second step. Once more, a wrong answer suggests the student needs more fundamental help.]

LESSON: Multiply the bigger number by 2 and enter your answer:
STUDENT: 16
[Had the student answered incorrectly, the program could infer that the student lacked the higher level prerequisite skill to use the lesson.]

LESSON: That's right. Does 3 go into this number without anything left over?
STUDENT: No.

LESSON: Multiply 8 by 3 and enter your answer:
STUDENT: 23

LESSON: No, think again. How much is 8 × 3?
[The lesson notes a multiplication error but can't say whether this shows a habitual weakness or just an isolated mistake.]

STUDENT: 24

LESSON: That's better. Does 3 go into this number?
STUDENT: Yes.

LESSON: Good. We're ready to go on. How much is 24 ÷ 3?
STUDENT: 8
             [Again, had there been an error, the lesson would have noted the weakness of student's basic math facts.]

LESSON: Now, you have to multiply the number over 3—the 1—by 8. How much is 1 × 8?
STUDENT: 8

LESSON: Now put that over 24 and you get 8/24. Let's do the same thing for the other fraction, ⅜. How many times does 8 go into 24? How much is 24 ÷ 8? . . .
             [The lesson continues following the algorithm until the student has been led to a solution. It concludes with a brief recapitulation of the steps involved. It also updates the model of the student to show what kind of errors were made.]

There is obviously a great deal more going on here than just an algorithm to add fractions. Two missing components, among others, are a tutoring strategy that makes instructional decisions and a model of the student. We will discuss both in subsequent chapters. For now, the point is that having a master performer of addition available gives the courseware the potential to prompt the student to do what the master performer would have done. Whenever a discrepancy arises between the master's and student's actions or whenever the student doesn't know what next to do, the lesson can advise by referring to the master performer.

The ability to know and advise marks the main difference between intelligent and scripted courseware. The latter concerns itself with the student's answer far more than with the process that produced it. Although in scripted courseware, we can use anticipated wrong answers to diagnose problems, such diagnoses tend to be coarse-grained, based as they are on final answers rather than on the procedures that gave rise to error. Intelligent courseware, on the other hand, takes the student step by step through the whole process the master performer uses so that the process itself could be learned.

WHY INCORPORATING ALGORITHMS INTO COURSEWARE IS DIffiCULT

Master performers—be they experts in doing addition, finding faults in electrical circuits, or parsing sentences—aren't easy to incorporate into teaching for a number of reasons:

Multiple solutions to the same problem   Often, more than one legiti-mate way exists to solve a problem. Which one do we choose? For example, a solution may be extremely elegant and still not be useful for teaching. Its very elegance can make it difficult for a novice to understand because what is logical and efficient for a computer may be mysterious for a human.

Constraining learning   Insisting on a master performer's way as the *only* way can inhibit the better student from following inspired guesses and sudden insights. The compensation is that the student at sea in a problem has something with which to keep from drowning.

Discovering algorithms   Discovering what master performers actually do is difficult. It's entirely common for great chefs or chess players or scientists or writers to work brilliantly while being at a loss to say what they're doing in terms that can show someone else how to perform as well. For example, we know how to write explicit instructions for solving linear equations; we are less successful in doing the same for problems posed by literature or philosophy. So while a correct result is assured with a properly constructed algorithm, there is no assurance that an algorithm can be properly constructed for every subject.

The discussion that follows about writing algorithms is not itself an algorithm but a "heuristic," or "quasi-algorithm." If one follows the advice offered, there is only a reasonable likelihood that a master performer will result, not an absolute guarantee. Indeed, the goal of a piece of courseware might be to teach only a heuristic. That is, it would show the student a general set of instructions that point toward a solution but leave some elements unspecified and uncertain.

The first two of these difficulties—multiple solutions and the con-straint on learning—are cautions about the appropriate use of master performers. The last is more practical: How does one create a master performer to use in courseware?

THINKING ALGORITHMICALLY

An algorithm is a clearly articulated set of instructions that, applied to the appropriate kind of problem, guarantees a correct and efficient solution. We can think of it as a recipe. When we bake cake, for instance, we first assemble ingredients; then we combine them and beat the mixture for so many minutes. Finally, we bake it in the oven at a specified temperature for a specified period of time. Each step of the recipe must have unambig-uous instructions, and all steps must fit together into a single, coherent sequence.

TWO TYPES OF ALGORITHMS

We can distinguish between two classes of algorithms, *procedural* and *analytic:*

Procedural algorithms follow clearly defined sequences of action (for example, to add numbers, calculate income tax, or operate equipment).

Analytic algorithms (sometimes called "declarative") articulate the attributes or features of some object (like a student's answer).

In practice, we usually solve complex problems with both procedures and analysis. Correcting a sentence, for instance, may require that one first analyze its constituent parts and then follow a procedure to make the necessary changes.

THE IF-THEN FORMALISM

Both types of algorithms use the IF-THEN formalism: If some condition (or set of conditions) is true, then we either take an action or make a deduction. By combining various conditions with actions, we can describe quite complex activities. IF-THEN constructions, also known as "production rules," have been used with intelligent computer programs and expert systems for such things as geological surveying and medicine, for example. We've seen the IF-THEN formalism already in the scripted courseware we have sampled. Now we will be using it for controlling not only the flow of a lesson but for describing the basic knowledge that the lesson teaches.

A PROCEDURAL EXAMPLE: WHAT DO I DO NOW?

Let's start with a procedural algorithm that goes through a math problem in a well-set-out sequence of actions. Figure 9.1 was the basis for the earlier conversation about fractions.

The function of this algorithm is to solve the problem of adding two fractions. The appropriate class of problems, therefore, is any involving the summing of two numbers such as ¼, ½, or ⅜. Like all procedural algorithms, it tries to keep answering a single question: "What do I do now?" The answer to that question changes as conditions change in the course of going through the procedure. At each juncture, the algorithm must be prepared to deal with any contingency that could arise. Let's try it out by entering ¼ and ²⁄₄.

Once we've passed START, we ask, "What do we do now?," the algorithm directs us to see if the two denominators are equal. If they are—as they are here—what we do now is simply add the two numerators and write the result over the common denominator:

$$1 + 2 = 3 = \frac{3}{4}.$$

And what we do now is stop because we've reached the solution. Of course, had the result been an improper fraction like 4/3, we might have been told to change it into a mixed number. But we'll save such refinements for other versions.

Let's use the algorithm with fractions whose denominators are not equal: ½ and ²⁄₄. Again, "What do we do now" is the question we'll ask

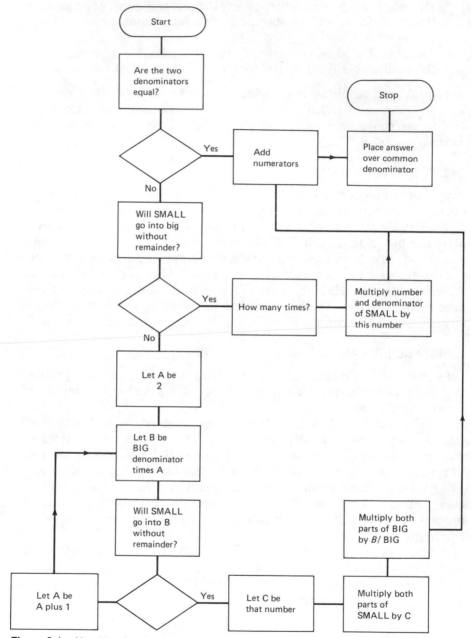

Figure 9.1 Algorithm for the Addition of Fractions

continuously. After we answer no to the query about equal denominators, the algorithm asks us if the smaller denominator (2) goes into the bigger one (4) without a remainder. ("Smaller" of course refers to the integer in the denominator, not the value of the whole fraction.) Since we answer yes to this, we are told to multiply both numerator and denominator of the smaller by the number of times 2 goes into 4. We do this, giving us $2 \times 1 = 2$ and $2 \times 2 = 4$ which we are told to arrange as $\frac{2}{4}$.

What do we do now that both fractions have the same denominator? We go back and do just as we did in the first case: Add the two numerators (2 and 2), place the result over the common denominator (4), and stop. In the earlier conversation between lesson and student, the algorithm was used in the more complex case of $\frac{1}{3} + \frac{3}{8}$. There, the master performer had to go through extra steps to convert the denominators before it could add them.

ANSWERING THE CENTRAL QUESTION OVER AND OVER

The key technique for writing procedural algorithms is relentlessly to keep answering the question "What do I do now?" We are not concerned at first with *why* something is done the way it is but *how* it can be done at all. Later on, the "why" can become the basis for selecting or refining an algorithm, but our first job is to construct one that works. Similarly, when we present an algorithm to students, we are less concerned at first with how much they understand and more concerned with how much they can do (for example, addition). Later on, we can move toward providing them with a deeper sense of what informs the algorithm.

When we write a procedural algorithm, the "What do I do now?" question must be anticipated even if its answer at some specific point won't be needed for one particular problem. We don't need to create variables A, B, and C when we add $\frac{1}{4}$ and $\frac{2}{4}$ or $\frac{1}{2}$ and $\frac{2}{4}$, but their presence is absolutely essential when we add $\frac{1}{3}$ and $\frac{3}{8}$. Such anticipation of contingencies and the dogged answering of "What do I do now" *before* it is even asked are the cornerstones of producing procedural algorithms.

AN ANALYTICAL EXAMPLE: WHAT ARE THE ATTRIBUTES OF X?

Let's now move from the master performer that follows a procedure to one that analyzes some stream of data like a student's answer. We can also use this kind of algorithm in lessons which teach students how to identify or classify various complex objects, such as insects or trees. We replace "What do I do now?" with "What are the attributes of X?," X being either

the answer we want the student to give, or
the student's answer itself

We have two objectives in performing this "attribute analysis":

1. to identify the key features of a correct answer (in effect, to build a model of it)

2. to determine the presence or absence of these features in the student's answer

This will allow us to infer what the student does or does not know. We'll refine "What are the attributes of X?" so that we'll know not only the attributes themselves but also

in what combinations they exist
in what order they can be

Let's illustrate by way of an algorithm that classifies humans so that we may identify one man in particular. Suppose I am to meet my Uncle Max at the airport but can't get there myself. The only person available is a rather literal-minded friend who has never seen Max. I must, therefore, give her a set of Max's attributes so that she can recognize him from among the many people arriving on the same flight. Figure 9.2 sets out those attributes so that my friend can perform a search process on each passenger, aborting it when it fails, and then proceeding to the next candidate.

The instructions begin with "Human in view?" since the most obvious attribute of Max is that he's human. If only Coke machines and electric-eye doorways are in sight, the process is put on hold.[1] With an affirmative answer to that first question, my friend next considers whether the human in view is a male, since that is the second key attribute of Max. Notice that the question implies a "negative attribute" of Max: If whoever is in sight is a woman, then she certainly cannot be my Uncle Max. Notice too that we are expressing attributes as binaries—yes or no, male or female. This is not an absolute requirement, but is useful for the sake of clarity and for halving the number of subsequent candidates. Later on, we'll look at situations where there are more than two possibilities and a "negative attribute"— one that means an attribute can't exist—will become important.

The next attribute refers to Max's race: He is a white male. However, the plane is arriving from Miami, and Max is sure to be well-tanned. The entry-level for using this algorithm must include an ability to distinguish between "white" as a racial characteristic and "white" as a color with some range of values. As with the first question, a negative answer aborts the current search and sends my friend looking for another candidate. The next question also yields two possible answers: Is the potential Max less than six feet tall? Again this implies another entry level skill, that of measuring. A "no" aborts the search here.

Having eliminated anyone not male, white, and under six feet (all critical attributes of Max), we move on to what the candidate wears. When drawing up my list here, I knew Max had certain preferences, but I could

[1] I could add that if no human were in sight and it were now an hour after the flight has landed, then my friend should leave. How comprehensive we make an algorithm depends on what we define as primitives, that is, knowledge we expect users to have before they use the algorithm. This requires specifying the entry levels of users so that we don't need to state explicitly that they should leave if there are no people left at the arrival area.

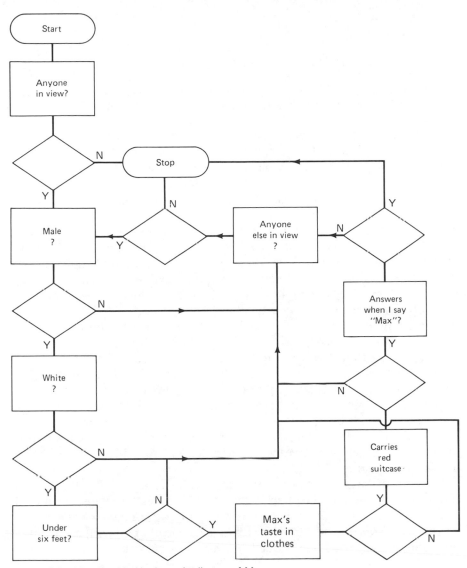

Figure 9.2 Meeting My Uncle or Attributes of Max

not be sure what they might be on any given day. The term "Max's personal tastes" may be broken down as follows:

Madras OR blue polyester slacks
AND
alligator T-shirt OR brightly colored-short sleeved shirt
AND
white belt

AND
white shoes
AND
(gold medallion OR love beads OR gaudy silver chain)
OR
gold medallion AND (love beads OR gaudy silver chain) OR (gold
  medallion OR love beads) AND gaudy silver chain

The list illustrates a key idea: attributes are combined "conjunctively" or "disjunctively." That is, they are placed into groups that either *may* or *must* include specified items. Max's shirt *may* have an alligator emblem or be short sleeved, but he *must* have a shirt. Similarly, he must have white shoes and white socks; his belt must be white; but his jewelry may be either a gold medallion or love beads or a silver chain or any combination. Jewelry he must have or he's not Max, but the sort and combination may vary.

The situation is the same for all Max's "personal tastes": Some attributes *must* be there, others *may* be there. In somewhat more formal terms, certain items by themselves are *necessary* but not *sufficient*; they must be there, but so too must others. Other things are sufficient in themselves; any one of a set of attributes joined by "or" will do. Constructing this list of attributes means specifying which possible combinations are acceptable if this is to be Max.

The rest of the algorithm follows the same pattern. He must carry a blue suitcase or a black one—a disjunctive combination. But suppose Max hates red—a negative attribute that would indicate that a white male under six feet tall dressed in "Max's personal tastes" and carrying a red suitcase could not possibly be Max. Having got this far, we ask the final question only of the best candidate: Are you Max? A no answer would abort this search and start another; a yes would end the search and Max would be on his way to my house.

The attributes listed in the Max algorithm are a model of the perfect (or at least acceptable) Max. Each would-be Max is tested against the model Max to see how well he compares. In the same way, a courseware master performer knows the ideal instance (or at least "nearly perfect") of the thing we want the student to have done. The student's answer is then compared to that ideal one.

To reiterate, the question that doggedly must be asked as we construct an analytic algorithm is not "What do I do now?" but "What are the attributes of X?"[2] That in turn is broken into three subquestions:

1. What are the conjunctive and disjunctive combinations of these
   attributes?

---

[2] We can refine it further by attaching degrees of certainty when we speak of attributes being present or absent. For instance, it is a 100% certainty that a Max candidate is human. Our certainty decreases, say to 90%, when we try to judge whether a candidate is taller than six feet. And it goes down even more if we try to pass judgment on "softer" items like personal taste in clothes.

2. What order must they follow?
3. What are the negative attributes, if any?

LOOKING AT STUDENT ANSWERS

Meeting Uncle Max—like adding fractions—may not be so complicated as to require this much explicitness. But the technique whereby he was identified is a powerful one that helps us say what the attributes of a correct answer should be and the line of reasoning that produces it. At the same time, the technique lets us ask what the attributes of a student's answer are and how they compare to the master's.

Here are a few examples of things a lesson could teach, more typical of courseware than meeting someone's uncle. The answer to the question "Express as a percentage the number of boys in a class of 30 in which 18 students are girls" has two attributes: the integer "40" and a percentage sign—and they must be in that order. If the question is changed to allow an answer in fractions or decimals as well as percentages, the attributes and their associations change too. Expressed as an IF-THEN statement, they become:

IF (40 and %) OR (. and 4) OR (12 and / and 30)
OR (4 and / and 10) OR (2 and / and 5)
THEN the answer is correct

Here a right answer can be made up of several more things than in the first instance, but they are permitted only in particular combinations. For example, a right answer clearly excludes a decimal point *and* a "30," even though both were parts of some other correct answers. They are correct only in combination with particular, specified elements but are mutually exclusive in the same answer.

Should an attribute of the student's answer be either *2.5* or *2½*, we have a negative attribute: Not only are the correct answers absent, but the one there shows the student has divided the total number of students (30) by the number of boys (12) rather than the other way around. If the answer were 60 percent (or .6 or 3/5), then we would have a negative attribute that showed the student used the number of girls (18) rather than the number of boys in his calculations.

We could continue adding to the list of negative attributes, choosing them to show the "bugs" we posit as being most likely to occur. Examining the stream of input from the students helps us decide on a specific piece of advice, suited to a specific misconception. We'll look at this sort of record keeping more fully in Chapter 10.

An Example From Music

The request "Give the notes in any major scale you like" produces a correct answer with the following attributes:

(C AND D AND E AND F AND G AND A AND B) OR
(D AND E AND F# AND G AND A AND B AND C#) OR
(E AND F# AND G# AND A AND B AND C# AND D) OR . . .

and so on for all the notes in all the major scales. In each case, only certain
combinations are possible, and they exclude anything else. However, in
certain keys like D major, the student might give (albeit not strictly correctly) the sharpened notes other names (like Gb or Db) which are
"enharmonic"; that is, they are actually the same sounds with different
names. One could therefore revise the D major scale this way:

D AND E AND (F# OR Gb) AND G AND A AND B AND (C# OR
Db)

The presence of these notes in students' answers tells us that they may not
be completely correct (the right keys but the wrong names) but at least they
are on the right track.

Some Brief Examples from the Social Sciences

The answer to "Name the three American presidents who preceded Ronald
Reagan and their political affiliations, beginning with the most recent"
would have the following attributes:

Carter AND Democratic
AND
Ford AND Republican
AND
Nixon AND Republican

A correct answer, therefore, would have two parts: a man's name and
a political party. Not only is the sequence of the whole answer crucial but
so is the combination of name and party. Had the question been phrased to
ask for the man's name with either his political affiliation OR his vice
president, the answer would have these attributes:

Carter AND (Democratic OR Mondale)
Ford AND (Republican OR Rockefeller)
Nixon AND (Republican OR (Agnew OR Ford))

The attributes of a correct answer to "Name three of the Great Lakes"
could be the whole set of possible combinations of their names or more
simply (because the question asks for no special order):

THREE of (Erie OR Huron OR Michigan OR Ontario OR Superior).

We can continue in this fashion in many areas, and it is good practice
to try the exercises at the end of this chapter. Building models of complex
domains is the first step in going beyond multiple-choice questions. With

them, we can examine the student's answer not merely for a single attribute but for several. That, in turn, leads to instructional decisions that better reflect the complexity of the subject and the variety of the student.

USING HEURISTIC STRATEGIES: WHEN WE CAN'T ALWAYS KNOW FOR SURE

Many times, we simply can't discover algorithms. Not every subject can be as neatly described as addition. Teaching someone about the ambiguities of language, for example, requires complex semantic understanding. So too for history, philosophy, and the fine arts. In such cases, the only instructional strategy available is a heuristic or broad problem-solving technique that guarantees neither an acceptable result nor even a particularly efficient path to that result. Typically, heuristics are used where some expert interpretation or fine-grained judgment is required—interpretation of context or of the likelihood that something is or isn't so.

Wheatley (1972) gives the example of bank officers who must decide whether or not to lend money. Their task involves more than just looking at a particular company's assets in relation to its liabilities. Successful lenders (those who reduce risk while attracting many customers) examine not only a borrower's current state of affairs but also past history and prospects for success if the loan were granted. Such judgments are not made in simple binary fashion (good or bad) but by a more fine-grained scale of levels of confidence. Although one may apply certain mechanical tests about the risk, the results are still interpreted by a human expert before a final decision gets taken.

USING MASTER PERFORMERS IN INTELLIGENT SUPPORT SYSTEMS

Heuristics can be the basis for intelligent support systems, which cannot themselves find answers but can help a student do that. An example of such a support system can be one for teaching punctuation. Its intelligence knows this heuristic (among others): A sentence containing a coordinate conjunction (*and, but, or, nor*) is properly punctuated:

> IF the coordinate conjunction joins two main clauses OR the last item in a series,
> THEN it must have a comma before it;
>
> IF the coordinate conjunction joins two coordinate objects,
> THEN it must not have a comma before it.

But the same intelligence can't say what exactly is being joined. That must be decided by a human because it involves semantic information that is either difficult or impossible to determine algorithmically. Specifically, one must know what constitutes a main clause. That in turn requires knowing what does or does not constitute a complete thought, which can be tricky.

To repeat the earlier example from linguistics: Is the phrase *Fruit flies* a declarative sentence that asserts that fruit can travel through space? Or is it simply a noun phrase, naming a species of insect? The answer can only be determined by a sense of the context in which the words are used. But determining context, although partially explicated by research in semantics and artificial intelligence, remains out of the reach for most writers of courseware.

LEARNING THROUGH HUMAN-MACHINE COOPERATION

Such problems don't mean we can't design courseware when we can produce only a heuristic for the master performer to follow. It does mean, however, a shift in how we describe courseware. If we suppose the computer to be the source of all knowledge and final arbiter, then a dead end certainly looms. However, if we instead see computer and student as cooperating actors in an exchange, it becomes possible for the student to help the computer when *it* needs help, instead of only the other way around.

In the case of placing commas, we should remember that human beings are excellent at seeing through semantic ambiguities. And since dealing with semantic ambiguity is where computers are weakest, it makes sense to allow the machine to ask for help from its human user. In turn, the humans can rely on the computer always to recognize coordinate conjunctions in sentences and look through the list of rules to determine how they are to be punctuated. When the applications of these rules require semantic information, the focus can turn back to the student.

What emerges is an "intelligent support system" instead of a tutor. However, if our objective is to teach a student to place commas—rather than producing a program with the intelligence to punctuate the sentence independently—then this is an unimportant distinction. The goal in writing courseware, we should note, is substantially different from writing AI programs which try to emulate general intelligence. AI places its focus on the machine and its capabilities. CAL, however, emphasizes the process of the student learning, regardless of how much the machine knows. The chapter on tutoring strategies will return to this issue, but for the moment, let's see how a master performer's combination algorithm and heuristic for punctuating coordinate conjunctions can be used.

THE STARTING POINT OF THE MASTER PERFORMER'S COOPERATION

We again begin with the attributes of a properly punctuated sentence expressed as an IF-THEN statement and then add the following instructions:[3]

---

[3] A properly punctuated sentence has in fact many more attributes than these; I limit them here just to illustrate.

IF a coordinate conjunction is not found, STOP.

If a coordinate conjunction is found, then display "Does the coordinate conjunction join two main clauses?"

IF student answers "yes", then display "Place a comma before the coordinate conjunction" and stop

IF student answers "no" then display "Does it join the last item in a series?"

IF student answers "yes", then display "Place a comma before it" and stop

IF student answers "no" then display "Does it join two coordinate objects?"

IF student answers "yes" then display "Don't place a comma before it" and stop

IF student answers "no", then display "There are no other possibilities" and go to a help module

The last contingency shows an inherent problem in depending on students: They may not have the requisite entry skills to use the program, and so their responses may not be correct. This is indeed a problem. However, if the lesson can prompt them so that they can express their uncertainty—they aren't sure if two main clauses are being joined—then it has at least discovered that they need extra help. How to give that help is a function of a tutoring strategy. For the moment, we should see that having incomplete information in itself does not necessarily preclude the development and use of courseware.

The punctuation heuristic is both procedural and analytic. We first do the attribute analysis as far as we can. For instance:

> If *and* or *but* or *or* or *nor* is present, then display "Does the coordinate conjunction . . . "

That done, we go on to the procedural part:

> If the coordinate conjunction does join two main clauses, then place a comma before it.[4]

By chaining a series of such searches for attributes together with actions to be taken should they be found, we can build up a complex set of instructions about grammar, syntax, and other kinds of punctuation. Naturally, the success of all this depends on how well the set of attributes and procedures we use for a task really reflects what an expert looks for and does. Creating that benchmark or model is the critical first step, and there is no algorithm to produce algorithms. There are heuristics, however, which we can frame as questions.

---

[4] Note that the "Then" portion can direct either the student or the computer to place the comma, depending on the instructional strategy. That is, we can show the student what the corrected sentence would look like by automatically inserting the comma, or we can ask the student to do it.

SELECTING AND ARRANGING ATTRIBUTES: SOME STARTING-POINT QUESTIONS FOR CREATING MASTER PERFORMERS

The courseware instructional design plan in Chapter 1 began by setting a goal, that is, a typical example of the class of problems we wish students to solve. Similarly, to develop an algorithm or heuristic for courseware, we first locate a model of what we wish to teach. Clearly, everything rests on how well the model problem meets the requirements of "typical." We can then ask a set of questions to elicit the key attributes. The list is not exhaustive, nor will it lead directly to code; it is intended only as a starting point:

- What attributes must *always* be present? What ones can *sometimes* be present?

Some attributes are always present (like breathing in a healthy person) and others are only sometimes present (like breathing in a critically injured person). We start, then, with what conditions are *necessary* and what conditions are *sufficient*. In several of our examples, attributes were joined either by AND or OR. Where AND was used, each individual attribute was *necessary*—the object could not be the object in its absence. But it was not *sufficient* because some other attribute also had to be present. In the percentage problem, both a particular integer AND a percentage sign were necessary, but neither by itself was sufficient for us to call the answer correct.

On the other hand, attributes joined by OR are both necessary and sufficient. That is, although we couldn't say that the object exists in their absence, only *one* such attribute is required for us to say it does exist. This allows students to answer in more than just one way. In the question about American presidents, for instance, the correct answer included either political affiliation *or* vice president.

- What form or state does the attribute have?

An attribute can have a physical property like color or weight. It also can be a state like "on" or "off" on a switch or "25" on a meter. It can indicate a relationship like cause ("If the drum is struck, a noise will be heard") or function ("If the square root of 9 is taken, the result is 3"); or time or space ("If 1 is here, 2 should follow"). We look for what can be measured in a single word.

- What question does an attribute answer?

Different attributes can provide us with different sorts of information. For example, if a word is an adverb, it might answer (among other things) the question "when?" If an attribute is a number, it tells us how much or how many. We want to know, therefore, what unique piece of information an attribute can give us.

- Is the attribute ambiguous?

Landa (1974) speaks of "univocal" and "equivocal" features (i.e., attributes). Univocal features are ones about which everyone agrees, things that can be easily quantified or recognized by shape, color, or dimension. One can easily discriminate univocal features from others. There are precise differences between, for example, a triangle and a circle, and everyone evaluates them in the same way. Equivocal features, on the other hand, ask us to be far more subjective. We can readily agree, for instance, that Max is a male; it is harder to get unanimous agreement about his taste in clothes. Clearly, an attribute analysis has the best chance if it identifies features that are less open to subjective judgments.

However, with an intelligent support system, we don't have to reject equivocal attributes automatically because we can call upon the user to provide the necessary interpretation. It goes without saying, of course, that one should try to identify features that are as unambiguous as possible. At the very least, potentially ambiguous features have to be recognized and marked as sources of possible confusion.

- Is the order of attributes important?

For some procedures, it makes no difference which parts are carried out first. For example, in adding a set of numbers like 3, 4, 5, and 6, we can start anywhere. However, this is not the case for a mixed calculation:

$$3 + (4 \times 5) - 6$$

yields a different result from

$$((3 + 4) \times 5) - 6$$

If an attribute must precede another in space or time, that order must be made explicit.

- What are the primitives?

Primitives are operations or facts so elementary that they do not themselves have to be explained. For instance, an algorithm that directs one to solve "2 + 2" will fail if the user doesn't know the meaning of either "+" or "2". An algorithm that asks "Is the first word a noun" will fail if the user doesn't know what a noun is or can't find out. Properly speaking, such failures lie not with the algorithm but with users insufficiently prepared to follow it. An appropriate entry level has to be specified. The same applies when we construct master performers in courseware: "Find a coordinate conjunction" is meaningless if the computer has not been first told what words are members of that class.

- Is everything accounted for?

This may sound platitudinous since no one will deliberately write an algorithm that doesn't account for everything. But it is a practical reminder to ensure that every possibility raised has been dealt with. If, for example, one is classifying all mammals, there must be a result for creatures with articulated thumbs who walk upright. There are two ways of accomplishing this. The first is to examine the algorithm in flow chart form and try to trace every possible path for loose ends. (Although other forms of representation are possible, the flow chart's graphics make such tracing relatively easy.) The second method is the purely experiential one in which the widest possible range of materials is fed into the algorithm or heuristic. Until failures emerge, we can work with the assumption of its completeness.[5]

The converse to completeness is irrelevancy. If the user is forced through a path that does not bear on the solution, the process is inefficient. Only those steps that are actually needed should be included. Again, this is tested by either tracing the flow chart or through experience with many users.

- Is this the most efficient question to ask here?

The most efficient question is the most general, the one that discriminates among the greatest number of possible cases. A rough test for this is whether or not the remaining possibilities are halved. For instance, a procedural algorithm that does taxes might ask, "Do you earn more than $50,000?" This is better than "Do you earn more than $50,000 but less than $100,000?" since the first yields only two groups and the latter three (under $50,000, less than $100,000, more than $100,000). One can group binaries, as we've seen, with AND and OR conjunctions to reflect complex associations.

- Does the process work?

Again, this may seem platitudinous, since no one will knowingly write an algorithm that doesn't work. But we can't neglect validating the algorithm so that we know it to be as general as we can make it. An algorithm may work in a few carefully selected places, but this is no guarantee that it is sufficiently robust for every case. The best way of making sure is to submit the algorithm to small- and large-scale testing, revising it as more information comes in. Even then, one that works may not be the only possibility. Indeed, validation is just a prelude to seeing how the algorithm can be made more efficient.

SUMMARY

Algorithms are step-by-step procedures that produce correct answers; heuristics are general guidelines with no such guarantees. Both allow us to build master performers in the areas we wish to teach. The solutions produced

---

[5] Strictly speaking, we cannot affirm an algorithm's completeness until absolutely every pathway has been explored. We can only say that the pathways we have explored are complete.

by master performers are the standards against which we compare student answers. The discrepancies that emerge allow us to make the necessary inferences to decide what instruction should follow. We develop algorithms:

1. to solve problems we ask students to solve
2. to examine the complex attributes in the stream of input from the student
3. to act as the basis for intelligent support systems

There are two broad categories of algorithms and heuristics: *procedural* and *analytic.*

1. Procedural answer the question "What do I do now?";
2. Analytic answer the question "What are the attributes of X?", X being a perfect or at least typical example or answer.

EXERCISES

These are pen-and-pencil exercises, not ones to be done at the computer.

1. Write procedural algorithms for the following:
   a. finding out a phone number in another city, making the call, and charging it to a different phone than the one you're using
   b. subtracting one five-digit number from another
   c. determining whether an object is a square
   d. calculating tax based on the these instructions:

"Taxpayers may deduct from their net income the funds paid into a pension fund 20% of their gross income up to a maximum of $3500. If they are members of a company pension plan, however, they must subtract the amounts paid by their employers from the 20% or $3500 when making their annual contribution." Express this law as an algorithm for persons in all categories, doing their taxes.

2. What are the attributes of the following:
   a. a list of monarchs of England in this century and the years they ruled
   b. the future tense of any regular French verb ending in "er"
   c. a Venn diagram showing that all men are mortal, Socrates is a man, and Socrates is mortal
   d. the Canadian maritime provinces going from west to east and their capital cities

REFERENCES

There is not a great deal of literature on writing educational algorithms and heuristics. The classic work is Landa (1974) but Gerlach (1975), though much shorter, also provides both strong theoretical background and practical examples. Gane (1967), Ryan (1970), and Wheatley (1972), all more directed to training rather than school situations, are very useful. Also recommended is the research in artificial intelligence which considers many of the same issues, albeit not from a purely educational perspective. Barr (1981) is a well-presented compendium of approaches, including an excellent summary of intelligent CAL. O'Shea and Self (1983) discuss the intelligence that informs a number of ICAL programs.

Barr, A. Feigenbaum, E. A., and Cohen, P. R., *The Handbook of Artificial Intelligence,* 3 vols. (Los Altos, Calif.: William Kaufman, 1981).

Gane, C. P., Horabin, I. S., and Lewis, B. N. "Algorithms for Decision Making," in Unwin, D., and Leedham, J. *Aspects of Educational Technology* (London: Methuen, 1967).

Gerlach, V. S., Reiser, R. A., and Brecke F. H. *Algorithms in Learning, Teaching, and Instructional Design.* (Technical Report 51201, College of Education, Arizona State University, Tempe, 1975).

Landa, L. N. *Algorithmization in Learning and Instruction* (Englewood Cliffs, N.J.: Educational Technology Publications, 1974).

O'Shea T. and Self, J. *Learning and Teaching With Computers* (Englewood Cliffs, N.J.: Prentice-Hall, 1983).

Ryan, W. S., Willis, V.A.C., Brook, P. W. *The Increasing Use of Logical Trees in the Civil Service.* (CAS Occasional Paper No. 13). (London: Her Majesty's Stationery Office, 1970).

Wheatley, D. M. and Unwin, A. W. *The Algorithm Writer's Guide* (London: Longman Group Limited, 1972).

chapter 10

Modeling the Student

IN THIS CHAPTER

- We go beyond recording only right and wrong answers to recording the process by which the student reaches those answers.
- We begin with informal models that ask the student to supply information. We then consider somewhat more rigorous models for scripted courseware, which group different types of responses.
- We then look at more formal models which take one of two basic strategies:
  1. *Buggy* models posit "bugs" or faulty procedures the student might have.
  2. *Overlay* models superimpose an image of the master performer's abilities on top of an image of the student's.
- Model building faces a number of serious problems:
  1. representing the domain we wish to teach and the various ways a student might fail to understand it
  2. conflicting information from the student, which makes it hard to isolate a particular fault
  3. the inconsistent ways students develop
- Finally, we consider a matrix notation for the student model.

THE NEED FOR STUDENT MODELS: DIFFERENT ROADS TO ROME

"An error," the psychologist Haim Ginott once advised teachers to tell their students, "is not a terror." These words do more than comfort learners. They tell instructors that student mistakes are not only inevitable but are also opportunities to discover where and why things go wrong in teaching. Knowing that is more important than knowing just the student's answer. Let's see why by way of a sentence that might be given to freshman composition students:

> That now is the time for men and women of good will and patriotism to come to the aid of their country, is evident.

While it is true that accomplished writers may disagree about where to place a comma, most composition texts agree this sentence should have no comma. Most writing teachers would probably also agree that before giving students license to disregard rules the way experts sometimes do, those rules have to be learned. Such logic dictates that we explain to novice writers that the comma in the sentence above is wrong because everything from the opening *That* to *country* is a noun clause that functions as the sentence's subject. When students incorrectly insert commas in sentences like this, they usually offer one of three reasons:

1. They believe that a comma lets the reader take a necessary breath.
2. They don't know what the subject is.
3. They aren't sure whether or not a comma is necessary when the subject is longer than a single word.

For each group of students, the instruction that follows must be quite different. The "comma-as-pause" students have formulated a wrong idea—a malrule as it is sometimes called—based on a false analogy with speaking. The students who don't see that the noun clause *is* the subject of the sentence need to know how to recognize what's there in front of them: noun clause, intransitive verb, predicate adjective. The last group, who weren't sure about commas when the subject was longer than a single word, need to be given a straightforward rule that the length of the subject is immaterial.

The point, quite clearly, is that although all three groups of students made the very same error, they did so for quite distinct reasons. If we know only that the error was made but don't know why, we have very little to go on when we try to decide what instruction should come next. As courseware designers, this means that we cannot consider only how many right or wrong answers the student has given or even the paths through the material. To do that is to focus only on an end product—the answer—rather than the process by which it was reached.

WHY TESTING ISN'T ALWAYS CONCLUSIVE

In many, many instances, answers don't reflect what a student knows. Here are some reasons why:

Multiple-choice questions give test-wise persons the chance to guess by eliminating alternatives until only a couple of plausible choices are left.

Constructed response questions offer no absolute proof of learning because facts can be memorized without being integrated into a body of knowledge. For example, knowing that an article of the constitution guarantees freedom of association does not necessarily mean one knows what is meant by association, why democracies permit it, or the history of its suppression.

Knowing how to substitute values into a formula does not mean one necessarily understands anything but simple math. Understanding Ohm's law, for instance, involves more than replacing the letters in $R = V/I$ with numbers.

CONTROLLING LEARNING REQUIRES A MODEL OF WHO IS LEARNING

Systems theory tells us that if we are to control a process (like the way someone learns a subject), we must have a model of that process.[1] Control in this sense doesn't imply an Orwellian world of moral coercion but an intentional ordering of instruction to make learning easier.

Students are complex systems, capable of generating much variety, especially in the ways they correctly or incorrectly reach their answers. We're unlikely to understand that variety in all its complexity by just looking at the end-product of an involved thinking process. If we want to instruct someone—which requires us to control a set of instructional events—we have to model the sorts of reasoning processes that each person uses or fails to use. This is difficult enough in a classroom where communication is fairly straightforward. In courseware, where we are removed from direct contact with the student, it is especially difficult. But it is no less critical for that.

PAST RESEARCH IN STUDENT MODELING

There have some notable efforts to build models of students, not as "optional extras" (Self 1979), but as central parts of courseware. First-generation lessons recorded, as many still do, simply right and wrong answers. But as early as 1962, Smallwood attempted to use correct answers as a guide to asking more difficult questions. In this, he was followed by Taylor (1968) and Peplinski (1970).

The first major modeling effort, however, came with Carbonell's (1970) "mixed-initiative" program to teach South American geography. What the program knew about geography was represented as a semantic network (a map of the relationships among the subject's topics). As the student accessed various topics in the course of instruction, the system tagged them, which

---

[1] This is a corollary of Ashby's "Law of Requisite Variety." (See Ashby 1964.)

allowed one to at least see what students had seen. Knowing that, of course, did not necessarily mean knowing what students had mastered but only what they had been exposed to.

A significant extension of Carbonell's work was Goldstein's (1979) "genetic graph" to coach students in the game of WUMPUS. The graph represented "evolutionary skills" (increasingly sophisticated ones, that is) needed to succeed at the game. By conservatively estimating a student's level, the lesson could give advice that was on the frontier of the current set of skills and so likely to be the most helpful.

Another highly sophisticated effort to model the student was O'Shea's (1979) "self-improving quadratic tutor." Models included statements of confidence that a "hypothesis tester" had in the student's mastery of rules for solving quadratic equations. By examining what rules had been learned and in what combinations, the program was able to attach estimates of success for other rules. Such estimates ranged from "Certainly" to "Certainly Not" with the crucial "Don't know" as well. (A program must know what things it doesn't know if it's going to avoid building a misleading student profile.)

Some early courseware used a technique, now mostly discarded, which made predictions based on statistical data about the meaning of particular answers. The implication was that learning follows some mathematical model; a student with a specific mistake should have a known probability of making another, similar error. If one could find such a model, then choosing new material would be only a question of plugging values into it. But human learners are a notoriously recalcitrant bunch when it comes to behaving with that much mathematical consistency or precision. Educational psychologists still do not have a mathematical model of learning with anything like sufficient complexity to capture what humans do.

However, numerical values have been used somewhat more successfully to establish confidence levels about what the student knows. For instance, GUIDON (Clancy 1982) trains doctors in prescribing antibiotics. It gives a numerical value, based on its own knowledge, on how likely it is that the student is correct. But numbers make up only a part of the whole in GUIDON, and certainly not the main part. (We'll examine GUIDON again in Chapter 11.)

Sleeman and Hendley (1979) taught nuclear resonance spectra, building models derived from the students' explanations of why they took the actions they did to solve problems. The premise was that rather than watching the system recount why *it* did what it did, students would be more actively involved if asked to introspect about and articulate their own actions. From natural language input by the student, the program extracted— or tried to with varying degrees of success—formal statements that were then compared to those of a "domain algorithm" working on the same problem. The results were used to model the student. However, student explanations were not always reliable, often omitting key sections of what had been done. Nonetheless, the notion of having the student introspect remains a tantalizing one since it gives the chance for communication between human and machine to become genuinely two-way. We'll look at that again in the next chapter.

PRACTICAL PROBLEMS IN MODELING

However, most courseware has not made these kinds of efforts. There are some powerful reasons why this should be, not the least being the sheer difficulty of knowing a subject well enough to know what to look for in a learner. But beyond that, Sleeman and Brown (1982) locate three major issues in the attempts to build adequate student models for courseware:

1. how to find out which of a set of multiple and necessary skills is lacking or faulty in a student's repertoire
2. how to deal with the combinatorial explosion of possible student errors one can posit
3. how to sift through "noisy data," or errors that don't result from systematic misunderstanding as much as from local errors like fatigue or inattention

All three issues prompt the same question: Given a sample of the student's mind, how can we infer what is and is not understood? Two main types of models—informal and formal—try to answer this question.

INFORMAL MODELS

Gathering Information by Asking

Informal models ask students questions even before the lesson begins instruction. We can't learn everything we'd like to know this way, but some useful information is there for the asking. For example, before the lesson, we can ask students:

What style of learning they like—they may prefer to dive into a topic anywhere at all or to go through it in step-by-step fashion
If they would rather read text than see graphics
If they already understand a given topic

Later on, we can ask students why they made a particular mistake, perhaps by presenting them with a menu of possible reasons:

Did they not identify something in the question?
Did they forget a rule or simply not know it?
Did the error result from carelessness?

The trouble with this approach is that students sometimes say they understand when they don't—either from genuine confusion, from trying to please, or from trying to get the lesson over with. But with mature or highly motivated students, we can rely more on their self-perceptions, at least until we have evidence that they are wrong.

Gathering Information by Pretesting

All students have some prior knowledge that their records and our pretests can reveal, even if such information is incomplete. If we ask 20 questions on a pretest, all we will get is 20 answers, not the thinking processes that went into them. However, that still can tell us something about where to start and what, at least at the outset, to leave out.

FORMAL MODELS: A BASIC START

Scripted, branching lessons offer a convenient starting place for seeing how to construct formal models, albeit limited ones. In general, such courseware looks for a single letter or single word, matching it against a pre-stored correct answer. Most typically, scripted courseware keeps records through the anticipated wrong answers it uses for remediation. Everyone is familiar with the "No, that is the capital of Botswana" response and its equally well-known counterpart, "No, that is the capital of Lithuania." Knowing that the lesson displayed these messages tells us what the student thought at that point. However, as we saw in the chapter on writing scripted courseware, there is a limit to the number of such responses that can be anticipated and stored.

Unfortunately, too many lessons keep track only of the current answer. Rather than building any ongoing sense of student skills, these lessons neglect the possibility that there may be a pattern to student's responses that can be exploited to choose further instruction. Ignoring this is like assuming that it is a brand-new student who responds to each question and that previous answers are meaningless.

If we ask a sufficient number of questions of the student, we might discern a pattern of misconceptions. In practical terms, this leads to the common technique of recording the path a student takes through the lesson. When students give certain answers, they are led to certain frames. The lesson can then create a profile that might indicate their strengths and weaknesses. The operative word surely is "might," but let's see how this notion works in principle.

GROUPING DISTRACTORS

Suppose a set of scripted questions requiring French translations of English verbs are so constructed that the same three kinds of mistakes are in every question. For instance, in asking the student to translate expressions like "I give" or "I would have given," the distractors could be written this way: Type I distractors always give the wrong verb, such as *prendre* instead of *donner*; Type II distractors always give the wrong tense; and Type III distractors always give the wrong ending for the person (*Je donnez* instead of *Je donne*).

The student who entered mostly Type I answers could be advised to go back and study basic vocabulary. The student with lots of Type II answers could be told to review the basic forms of tenses. And the student with mostly Type IIIs could be told to review the endings for different persons.[2] This supposes, however, that the student will give responses sufficiently homogeneous for us to see a pattern emerge.[3]

GROUPING CONCEPTS

Another record-keeping tactic, useful both for tutorials and drill-and-practice, is to group questions by concepts. For instance:

> In lessons on grammar, we could record all the questions missed on capitalization or spelling or subject-verb agreement. This could be true both for mini-criterion tests at the end of each unit of instruction and for the test at the end of the whole lesson.
>
> If during the course of instruction the percentage of right answers fell below a certain level (for example, 80 percent), the lesson could decide to send the student to remediation frames for that particular concept.
>
> Similarly, records could be kept so the final score could be broken down into specific problem areas, and the student asked to go through just those parts of the lesson again or get help from the teacher.

Keeping records by concepts or skills mastered is obviously a better strategy than merely keeping aggregate scores. "You scored 50% on this test" isn't really helpful to the student or the teacher trying to decide which half of the material needs reviewing. But there still remains the fundamental limits of the basic strategy: We look only at the end result of the student's work, not at the means by which he reached it.

As O'Shea and Self (1983) point out, one can account for the longevity of this kind of record-keeping by remembering the behavioral roots of courseware in programmed learning. Combine those roots with the relative ease with which right and wrong answers can be collected, and we have a strategy that persists.[4] But longevity does not mean adequacy. To repeat: What courseware designers need to do is to turn record-keeping away from merely noting right and wrong answers toward thinking how those answers came about in the first place. Several possibilities exist.

---

[2] We naturally have to keep track of what choices presented what type of error. A list of each type and its various locations has to be maintained by the lesson.

[3] Carbonell's geography program, mentioned earlier, is a more sophisticated rendering of this strategy because the topics accessed by the student give a picture of what the student has seen of a domain.

[4] Historically, there were also storage limitations that made it difficult to do sophisticated record keeping. That clearly is no longer true. Record keeping may be time-consuming but it's not technically beyond current hardware.

BUGS: A MAJOR STEP IN FORMAL MODELS

In a classic pioneering paper, Brown and Burton (1978) proposed the "buggy" model in which a student's error points to a bug in the procedure used to solve a problem.[5] For instance, a student may produce this:

$$
\begin{array}{r}
501 \\
-\ \ 65 \\
\hline
564
\end{array}
$$

The answer suggests that the student has taken the smaller number from the bigger one in every column, regardless of whether the smaller number was on the top or on the bottom. Brown and Burton identified a hundred or so such bugs in subtraction. The program would look at a student's incorrect answer and then try the same subtraction problem, inserting various of these bugs into its own calculations until one was found that produced the same results as the student's. From this, the program could infer the procedure that students had followed and, importantly, could predict the exact digits they would write down in a new but similar problem.

THE DIFFICULTIES IN THE BUGGY APPROACH

At first blush, the buggy model appears straightforward, not only for teaching subtraction but for any area in which students follow an unambiguous procedure. One need merely think of all possible bugs in that procedure and run them (that is, solve the same problem the student tried) whenever the student gives a wrong answer. There are a number of complications, however:

> Not every bug can be predicted. Errors sometimes occur from "noise"—students not paying attention or just being tired.
>
> Students may not follow the same faulty procedure from problem to problem.
>
> Different bugs can produce the same wrong answer (just as we saw in the faulty comma example at the beginning of this chapter). Which one to select?
>
> Procedures may be made up of subprocedures, any one of which—say, a subtraction fact like 10−7=3—could be faulty. Isolating the subprocedure causing the error can require that all combinations of right and wrong subprocedures be tested. And this, not unlike the problem facing script-based courseware, means that eventually the possible combinations become so vast that there's just not enough time to run them all and their variations.

A general solution to these problems is to develop a set of heuristics to isolate the underlying cause for errors. Here are a few examples:

[5] Similar work, though not using computers, appears in Ashlock 1976.

If several bugs might produce the same behavior, one might consider only one or two. The most common bugs could be tried first, generating answers to problems and comparing them to the student's.

If there are two possible bugs, it may make no difference which order we think about them. So we can arbitrarily pick one to run through the problem the student missed.

If the results of the first bug affect the second, then the order *is* important. For instance, we might say, "If both the first and second bugs in a two-part procedure are there, generate problems to show each of them separately."

There can be several other confounding factors as well. A student may have a bug that doesn't interfere with getting the right answer in one particular problem. This would throw off any predictions since we might think no bug at all existed. We need heuristics to make explicit what constitutes this and other shaky evidence so we can generate the right type of problem and be sure what the student can or cannot do. But the process is time-consuming since we generally have to proceed through trial and error rather than through a prior, all-inclusive model of possible learner errors.

STUDENT MODELS REQUIRE EXPERT MODELS FIRST

It also quickly becomes obvious that the success in thinking of the student as someone who follows procedures that don't work first requires thinking of what procedures do work for an expert. Once more, we face the issue that we need mastery of a subject before attempting to design lessons to teach it. We can think of that expertise as a master performer to whom we compare the student, and it is this notion that provides us with our next formal modeling technique.

THE OVERLAY MODEL

The *buggy* model focuses on what the student can do wrong; the *overlay* model focuses on what the master performer can do right. An overlay model (the term is first found in Goldstein 1979) superimposes an image of a student's performance over what a master would do in the same circumstances. In effect, we view the student as an apprentice who has some but not all of the master's skills. Where the two differ is where we direct remediation. Figure 10.1 shows part of the path a master might take to solve a problem and a path of a student who deviates from it.

The overlay model is best used wherever there is an algorithmic solution to a problem. That is, if we have a large problem whose solution can be reached by taking a precise set of intermediate steps, each one we identify can be a source of error for the student. Rather than revealing merely wrong answers, the overlay model can capture the process by which

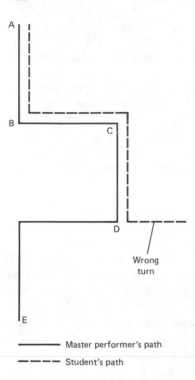

Master performer's path
Student's path

Figure 10.1 The Overlay Student Model

students reached their wrong answers. It's not unlike looking for the nail on the mule's shoe, the loss of which cost the shoe, which cost the wagon, which cost the battle. For if we can reconstruct the path the student follows, we may find that all but one skill was in fact mastered; we can then trace the wrong answer back to a specific wrong turn.

We should note that the path we speak of here is different from the frequent courseware technique of tracing the path of answers through a lesson. The overlay model is not concerned with a series of answers but with one particular answer and how the student produced it.

PROBLEMS WITH THE OVERLAY MODEL

There are several problems in using the overlay model, some of which we touched on in the chapter on master performers:

What can be modeled   There is the fundamental difficulty in getting skilled performers in any field to articulate what they do so that it can become a set of tasks that can be programmed by computers and then taught to students. Whenever a skill is highly developed, it often becomes so automatic to its possessor as to be almost inaccessible to his conscious mind.

Which expert to model   A problem often can be solved by several different methods. There is more than one way to do long division, more than one way to fly an airplane, more than one way to parse a sentence, even if the final results are all the same. Which method to use is a difficult decision because each may vary not only in computational efficiency but also in the ease with which one learns it. That is, many expert systems use algorithms that work perfectly well when run on a computer but are nonetheless impossible for human users to follow. The SOPHIE program, for example, analyzes faults in electrical circuits but uses a logic alien to humans. If our objective simply is to trace the fault in an electronic circuit (SOPHIE's area of expertise), there is no issue; but if the object is to teach someone to do the same, the logic must be readily grasped by people.

How often to model A third problem is one also faced by the buggy model: the one-swallow-does-not-a-summer-make syndrome. Does any single mistake provide sufficient data for us to assume that we've identified *the* difficulty?

For example: Students may not follow an algorithm because they may be tired or inattentive. It is also possible that they have not fully internalized the order of steps that constitutes the entire algorithmic procedure the overlay model assumes. We can teach and test for mastery of individual subskills and be satisfied that they're all in place. However, this doesn't necessarily mean that the student will be able to recall what next to do in a problem situation or which skill to draw on. Any program, therefore, that depends on modeling students as they follow an algorithm must first be sure that they have truly learned the structure of the whole algorithm and not just its constituent parts.

KEEPING RECORDS OF RECORDS

Record keeping requires a useful notation. There are a number of possibilities, depending on the kind of model we build.

Aggregate records If we count only the number of right answers, we need nothing more complicated than a variable that we increment each time the student is right. The same basic technique holds for keeping track of errors. Even if we go further and group errors by the type of skill or type of concept being taught, we still need only a single variable for each, incremented by one at the appropriate time. For example, we could have a variable called *Score* or others called *Spelling* and *Commas.*

When we combine looking at these variables with keeping track of the total number of questions asked, it is trivial enough to determine if the student has reached a given level of mastery (say 90 percent). But variables like these are rather crude measures of the student. To reiterate, they record only the result of thinking, not the process.

Recording process To record the thinking process requires a notation that looks at two things:

> How students fare at each juncture of an individual problem
> How they do over a period of time

By "juncture," we mean a place on the expert's path from which students can deviate. But a single example comparing a student's path with an expert's isn't likely to prove whether that skill is there or not. We have to track, therefore, how students do at more than just one try at solving the type of problem at hand. These tries may cover one session or many.[6] It is an open question how many different problems to give the student so that we can be confident of a diagnosis. However, it surely is more than a single one, and our notation has to show that.

Recording types of errors   It's also likely that any interesting area (even one as apparently simple as subtraction, as Brown and Burton [1978] show) has many types of potential errors or deviations from the master performer. A single problem will not be able to elicit their full range. We could use a different variable for each type of error; the vector notation that follows, however, is a less cumbersome way.

VECTOR NOTATION

The notation we need, then, must show three things:

> Each possible error or deviation from the master performer
>
> Whether or not the student shows mastery on a particular skill and how those skills develop over a period of time
>
> For which skills we lack sufficient data. It is just as crucial to know what we don't know about a student as it is to know what she ought to know herself

One such way to do this is to represent the domain we're teaching as a vector of 1s, 0s, and −1s. We reserve one slot in this vector for each identifiable skill in the master performer's algorithm. We proceed this way:

1. Initially, we set all elements of the vector to 0, there being as many elements as potential steps or items in the algorithm.
2. When the student attempts a problem, we match each step or item against what the master would do.
3. If both student and master do the same thing, we mark that element in the student model as 1.
   If there is a discrepancy, we mark it as a −1.
   If the particular juncture on the algorithm isn't accessed, we leave the corresponding element as 0. (A point not accessed decidedly is not the same thing as an error; a particular problem just may not require a particular step.)

---

[6] Maintaining a history of previous sessions and previous difficulties is important. A lesson could check, for example, if the student really mastered subtraction facts before going on to mixed calculations.

A vector containing the student record might look like this:

$$1\ 1\ 0\ -1\ 0\ 0\ 1\ 1\ 0\ -1$$

There are ten elements here, showing ten possible steps. Those marked with 1s show that the student's actions matched the master performer's and those with −1s show where the student made an error. Just as important as these, however, are the 0s, which tell us that a particular skill was never tested. We cannot say one way or the other if the student knows or doesn't.

By grouping vectors, each one representing one attempt or one problem, into matrices that show how the student does over many problems, we can represent skills in a particularly revealing way. Such a matrix might look like this:

	Col 1	Col 2	Col 3	Col 4	Col 5	Col 6	Col 7	Col 8	Col 9	Col 10
Row 1	1	1	0	1	0	0	1	1	0	−1
Row 2	1	1	−1	0	−1	1	1	1	1	1
Row 3	1	1	−1	0	−1	−1	1	1	1	0

Each row represents an attempt to solve a different problem of the same class. Each column represents the same skill over several problems. Looking at columns 1 and 2, we see that the first and second skills in the master performer's algorithm were present and successfully accomplished in all three samples (1, 1, 1, and 1, 1, 1). The third column (0, −1, −1) shows a skill, however, that was not tested the first time but in the second and third problems was done incorrectly. The fourth column (−1, 0, 0) shows that the only time we have information about the student's ability was on the first problem. We continue through these columns until we have identified where the student is weak or strong and (importantly) where we just don't know.

TAKING DECISIONS BASED ON STUDENT MODELS

Such information permits us to make very specific instructional decisions:

A column with a series of −1s tells us quite clearly that we should remediate that skill.

A series of −1s, followed by a few 1s, tells us the problem may once have been severe but now isn't.

A single −1 may tell us there's a problem that may require only a brief bit of help.

Two consecutive −1s may tell us the problem is increasingly serious and we should give more extended remediation.

A set of 0s might induce us to give the student a problem to elicit the information we lack.

In brief, we can construct a set of specific instructional plans based on what we find in the student matrix.

PROGRAMMING CONSIDERATIONS

In terms of computers, the matrix has a number of advantages.

> Most computer languages can put information into a matrix and then retrieve it quite rapidly. List-oriented languages like LOGO, where matrices are not supported, can represent the same information as a list of lists. The third element of every list, for example, can always refer to the same skill, just as does the third column in a matrix.
>
> The memory overhead of keeping 1s, 0s, and −1s is relatively low, meaning that even modest systems can store fairly big matrices, calling them back from disk when the student begins a new session. This permits past performance to be used conveniently and fairly quickly.

A CONCRETE EXAMPLE: AN OVERLAY MODEL AND MATRIX NOTATION

Let's examine a concrete example of student modeling, using a lesson that teaches punctuation of introductory clauses. Again, we assume that teaching punctuation may mean teaching rules that not every expert writer will agree with. However, students who have to write clear discursive prose need the unambiguous directions such rules provide.

The master-performer procedure we'll use begins by looking at the first word in a sentence and checking whether it is a subordinate conjunction, a preposition, an interjection, "yes/no," or a conjunctive adverb. Each one of these indicates that the subject of the clause does not come at its very start; one should place a comma before the subject, therefore, to avoid a possible misreading.[7] Let's further assume that the lesson can also physically shift a group of words to the end of the main clause and show the results to the student. If the sentence still makes sense after shifting a group of words, we know that the shifted element is introductory.

The lesson begins, then, by

1. looking for either the presence or absence of any one of the class of words above
2. shifting a group of words to see whether those words constitute an introductory element

The program must next look ahead and see if there is a comma in the rest of the sentence. If there is, it has to determine whether or not the comma comes just before the subject.

The Master Performer's Vector

Given a sentence like "Before they arrived at the dance, the ladies were excited," a vector showing the master performer's algorithm would look like this:

---

[7] As in "Above the sun shone brightly," where the reader has to reread to know that nothing is above the sun.

$$1\ 0\ 0\ 0\ 0\ 1\ 1$$

The 1 in the first position indicates that the sentence begins with a subordinate conjunction ("Before"); the following four 0s show that it does not begin with either a preposition, interjection, yes/no, or a conjunctive adverb. (The order in which these things are noted isn't important as long it's consistent.) The second-to-the-last 1 shows that the sentence does contain an introductory subordinate clause that could be moved to the end of the main clause, as in "The ladies were excited before they arrived at the dance." And the final 1 shows that a comma follows the introductory element.

The Student's Vector

Let us now look at the sentence as punctuated by a hypothetical student who knows that "before" is a subordinate conjunction but does not know the rules for testing and punctuating introductory adverbial clauses:

$$1\ 0\ 0\ 0\ 0\ -1\ -1$$

Like the master punctuator, the student can recognize what "before" is. However, on the basis of this exchange alone, we don't know if he could recognize prepositions, interjections, conjunctive adverbs, or "yes/no" as indicators that there is an introductory element. The penultimate −1 shows that the student has not requested a test by shifting the adverbial clause to the end. The last element shows us that he does not know the rule for inserting a comma after the adverbial clause.

Taken together, this information is still fairly partial. It can, however, be extended over two dimensions:

> We can add elements to this vector to reflect other skills: punctuating nonrestrictive elements, agreement of pronouns and their antecedents, and so on. The result would be a long vector made up of shorter ones. Each short one would show how students did on a single skill, while the long one would show how they did on a whole sentence.

> We can consider the current vector about introductory elements as just a single row of information that we'll add to others in a matrix as the student punctuates more sentences.

Here is what a student's matrix might be after three sentences:

$$1\ 0\ 0\ 0\ 0\ -1\ -1$$
$$0\ 0\ 0\ 0\ 0\ \ 0\ \ 0$$
$$0\ 1\ 0\ 0\ 0\ \ 1\ \ 1$$

Each row tells us about one sentence, and we've already looked at the first. The second row tells us that in the second sentence, there was no introductory element at all, and so gives us no information about punctuation skills or their absence. The third row tells us that not only can the student put the punctuation in the right place, but he can do so with prepositional phrases as well (assuming that the second column indicates that the sentence begins with a preposition).

Whether we look across the rows to find out about a single sentence or down a column to see how the student's skills are developing over several sentences, the vector notation gives useful information, including that which says we simply don't know enough to make a judgment about what the next unit of instruction should be.

SUMMARY

In this chapter, we looked beyond the need simply to record right and wrong answers toward a courseware that would reconstruct the process by which the student reached those answers. Informal models, easy to implement but not always reliable, ask the student to supply information such as preferences or current understanding. Somewhat more rigorous models in scripted courseware build models of students by structuring questions so that types of responses are grouped. We can direct the student having a great many wrong answers of one specific type to the appropriate remediation. More formal models yet take one of two basic strategies: "Buggy" models posit faulty procedures the student might have, and then attempt to solve problems using these bugs. "Overlay" models superimpose an image of the master performer's abilities on an image of the student's, seeing deviations as the key to providing further instruction.

Model-building faces a number of serious problems:

1. Representing the domain we wish to teach and the various ways a student might fail to understand it
2. Confronting conflicting information from the student, which makes it hard to isolate a particular fault
3. The inconsistent ways students develop

Finally, in this chapter, we considered a matrix notation for the student model.

REFERENCES

Ashby, W. R. *An Introduction to Cybernetics* (London: Methuen, 1964).

Ashlock. *Error Patterns in Computation,* 2nd ed. (Columbus, Ohio: Charles E. Merrill, 1976).

Brown, J. S. and Burton, R. "Diagnostic Models for Procedural Bugs in Mathematical Skills," *Cognitive Science,* 2 155–198 (1978).

Carbonell, J. "AI in CAI: An Artificial Intelligence Approach to Computer-Assisted Instruction," *IEEE Transactions On Man-Machine Systems.* MMS–11 (4) (December 1970).

Clancy, W. J. "Tutoring Rules for Guiding A Case Method Dialogue," in Sleeman, D. and Brown, J. S. *Intelligent Tutoring Systems* (London: Academic Press, 1982).

Goldstein, I. "The Genetic Graph: A Representation for the Evolution of Procedural Knowledge," *International Journal of Man-Machine Studies,* 11 (1979), 51–87.

O'Shea, T. "A Self-Improving Quadratic Tutor," *International Journal of Man-Machine Studies,* 11 (1979), 97–124.

O'Shea, T. and Self, J. *Learning and Teaching With Computers* (Englewood Cliffs, N.J: Prentice-Hall, 1983).

Peplinski, C. *A Generative CAI Program That Teaches Algebra* (Technical Report no. 90, Computer Science Department, University of Wisconsin, Madison, 1970).

Self, J. A. "Student Models and Artificial Intelligence," *Computers and Education,* 3 (1979), 309–12.

Smallwood, R. D. *A Decision Structure for Teaching Machines* (Cambridge, Mass: MIT Press, 1962).

Sleeman, D. H. and Brown, J. S. *Intelligent Tutoring Systems* (London: Academic Press, 1982).

Sleeman, D. H. and Hendley, R. J. "ACE: A System Which Analyses Complex Explanations," *International Journal of Man-Machine Studies,* 11 (1979), 125–44.

Taylor, E. F. "Automated Learning and Its Discontents," *American Journal of Physics,* 36 (1968), 496.

chapter 11

Courseware Tutoring Strategies

IN THIS CHAPTER

■ We examine a series of tutoring metaphors for courseware that say when a lesson should intervene. We begin with two that are at opposite ends of the courseware continuum:

- *Student control* permits students to choose whatever topics they wish when they wish; its weakness is that it may not give the student sufficient direction.
- *Author control* of instructional decisions is most often found in scripted courseware; its weakness is that it may not sufficiently take into account individual patterns and variety of learners.

■ More intelligent courseware takes a middle ground, both intervening and giving students an active role in choosing how learning proceeds. Examples of these strategies are:

- *Socratic:* a questioning tutor tries to impel students to see their mistakes;
- *Reactive learning environment:* the lesson reacts to student questions and hypotheses by simulating the effects of student ideas and presenting their implications.
- *Computer coach:* the lesson looks over the shoulder of students, offering advice at appropriate moments.
- *Intelligent assistant:* the lesson acts as a participant in a conversation with the student, seeking to reach understandings with the student about concepts in a particular subject.

■ The intelligent strategies are rule-based; that is, courseware design includes explicit rules for taking instructional decisions.
■ All strategies face three major problems:
  1. Courseware has difficulty finding out from the student what it needs to know, and so instructional decisions are based on partial and inferential knowledge.
  2. Courseware generally lacks a natural-language interface; this makes it difficult to communicate with the student.
  3. There is not a general theory of instruction that can tell courseware what to do at any given moment.

MAKING TUTORING EXPLICIT

If we know something about a subject and something about a student learning it, how can we use that knowledge in a tutorial? In previous chapters, we examined ways of representing master performers and ways of representing students who were trying to emulate these experts. To the degree that we've been successful in doing this, we are ready to combine both kinds of information and construct a dialogue between student and computer. We face a number of difficulties:

A limited channel for talking with students   It is difficult to have an ever-reliable communication channel between computer and student. Even the most crowded classrooms give the chance for teacher and student to clear up questions about what is being understood and what isn't, even if such exchanges aren't always frequent. However, courseware works at some remove from students, having to make inferences about what they know rather than asking them directly. Such inferences are based on incomplete knowledge far more often than in the classroom. As we saw in the chapter on student modeling, even right answers don't necessarily give enough or correct information.

A limited way to talk   A second major hurdle in designing courseware dialogues is the difficulty computers have with natural language. Despite much, much effort over thirty years, workers in artificial intelligence are still far from providing useful (let alone foolproof) ways for humans and machines to talk to one another. The most successful natural-language processors can do some impressive things in carefully chosen and restricted areas. But they have not solved the general problems of linguistic competence needed by courseware that truly simulates a live tutor. To do that, we have to make human contexts available to computers, and no one has really succeeded yet. (See Winograd, 1984, for an excellent account of the obstacles.)

But even if the most advanced of today's natural language processors were available, its hardware requirements would still be a limiting factor, despite a world of falling prices and increasing computer power. Hardware constraints will ease in time, but solutions to the programming problems involved in incorporating natural language processors into courseware will take considerably longer. Whatever the future brings, therefore, today's courseware designers have to work around the gap between what students could say and what they are allowed to say. This means making do with subsets of natural language that both designer and learner agree to use. In practice, lessons look for key words and phrases in student answers, extrapolating meaning from them.

    The lack of a theory of instruction   Perhaps the greatest problem in designing courseware is the one faced by all teachers: the lack of a general theory of instruction. How humans learn is still very much a matter of speculation, although certain areas have been usefully investigated. But fundamental principles of how things should be taught on a computer still remain largely unknown. To use a medical metaphor, we don't know how to prescribe the right doses of the right drugs at the right moment and be reasonably sure of their right effects. Much of what we do remains decidedly *ad hoc;* we try out ideas a bit at a time, guided more by a combination of observation and intuition than by a general theory that accounts for what we think is happening.

TUTORING STRATEGIES: A CONTINUUM OF INTERVENTION

A tutoring strategy implies intervention: Given some set of circumstances (a wrong answer, a perfect mark), a tutor should do something (remediate, go on to a new topic). Most courseware leaves primary control to the author. Some courseware, however, asks whether we need intervention at all. People, after all, often learn a lot at libraries, choosing books without much direction about how to understand what's in them. Why not extend this idea to courseware and, rather than have the lesson intervene, create a set of lessons that allows students complete freedom over what they're going to learn next? The computer, instead of being the final arbiter, becomes something like a librarian, making materials available and managing their distribution.

STUDENT CONTROL OF INSTRUCTION

The "student-control" approach has been used in various CAL projects and offers several apparent advantages:

> The major issue that we are thinking about in this chapter—intervention—becomes a nonissue. We no longer have to worry about what instruction to pick next since that is, by definition, the student's responsibility.

> The various modeling techniques and the problem of tracking

the student's progress become less critical. How fast to go, what topics to cover, what paths to follow—all become easy to resolve because they're somebody else's problem: the student's.

Student control is also attractive to educators who think computers should provide environments to be explored rather than directions to be followed.[1] One can accept or reject that view, but once the decision has been made to tutor via the computer, it's as necessary to articulate what we do in courseware as in the classroom. Indeed, a completely pure form of CAL—an environment with absolutely no intervention—isn't a tutorial system at all.

TICCIT: TRYING OUT STUDENT CONTROL

Perhaps the most ambitious effort to date to test student-controlled tutorials has been the TICCIT project (Merrill et al. 1980). TICCIT does have an advising capacity, but it's generally limited to telling the student what a topic's prerequisites are, showing sample test items, and describing materials. Its advice is essentially the same for all students. In fact, TICCIT's designers reject "the dream of a maximally adaptive system" that would assess a student's learning style, aptitudes, past achievement, and readiness. They argue that "a totally adaptive system, if it could be developed, would be maladaptive, making students . . . spoonfed." Since the natural environment is itself not adaptive, a "horrible nightmare" of overly dependent people might result: "When a student learns to select the next-best display on the system, he or she is also learning how to select the next-best display in noncomputer situations."[2]

The position adopted by TICCIT's designers implies transference: Learning to pick the next right thing in TICCIT helps one choose the next right thing in some other context. However, students who had used TICCIT for learning English grammar—and who scored in the high 80s on the lessons' posttests—still received essay grades that remained fairly steady at about C–. One can only conclude that letting students choose their displays may provide some short-term results, but skills are not transferred to new contexts like essay writing. Indeed, the TICCIT designers themselves conclude that performance was not as outstanding as they had hoped and that "the model needs to be expanded to handle evaluation and advisement of students with different learning abilities, levels of experience with course content, learning styles, and levels of motivation."[3] In brief, what's lacking is a student model and a tutoring strategy to respond to its implications.

The importance of the TICCIT experience is that student control was given an extensive, thorough, and sophisticated trial. Despite those efforts, the results indicate that just as a teacher has to intervene to make learning

---

[1] Seymour Papert and the LOGO movement generally subscribe to this view (see Papert 1980).

[2] Merrill et al. 1980, p. 10.

[3] Ibid., 126.

faster and easier, so too must tutorial courseware. That students eventually may learn on their own is true, but it doesn't follow that teaching is merely waiting for that to happen.

THE OTHER EXTREME OF INTERVENTION: AUTHOR CONTROL

If student control is one possible approach, giving full control to the lesson is another. Most scripted courseware works this way, following a scenario that the designer hopes will anticipate what students need. Unlike a play or movie script, however, the action varies, based, of course, on the answers students give as they go through the lesson. As we saw earlier, the designer tries to predict the most common responses to questions and route the student accordingly. But as we also saw, that approach is profoundly limited. Students become rather passive observers of their education, not participants, with the expression of their complexity often reduced to picking a single letter.

Even the best of such courseware can include only a fairly crude model of students, based solely on answers rather than the thinking that produced them. Lessons quickly get unwieldy when the designer tries to add more alternatives but still has to cope with the combinatorial explosion of answers and paths. However, despite the limitations of the scripted paradigm itself, there has been research that helps designers improve parts of it.

CHOOSING THE APPROPRIATE DISPLAY

Gagne and his associates (1981), for instance, have proposed a system for improving the display portions of scripted courseware. Each type of learning outcome, they argue, requires a different type of display. The designer's first job, therefore, is to classify what kind of learning the lesson intends. For example, teaching verbal information, defined or concrete concepts, rules, or problem solving all require different kinds of displays for the necessary "learning events" to work well. These events include the following:

1. gaining attention
2. informing the learner of the lesson's objective
3. stimulating recall of prior learning
4. presenting stimuli with distinctive features
5. guiding learning
6. eliciting performance
7. providing informative feedback
8. assessing performance
9. enhancing retention and learning transfer

"Gaining attention" can range from simply showing the word "Look" to asking a hypothetical question. "Stimulating recall" can be asking students to remember applicable rules or showing them maps and figures. Which display to choose is a function of what the courseware tries to accomplish at various points.

Gagne and his associates argue that designers have to pay attention to each of the events, although the final form of the courseware may not necessarily include them all. The value of this approach is that it tries to formalize what should be in the display portion of the program. The system, however, makes no suggestions about scripted courseware *per se,* and although the work suggests significant improvement, we are still left with the basic problem of scripted courseware: The student's variety is not given its fullest expression.

The author-controlled approach, with its roots firmly in programmed instruction, has been by far the most usual form of courseware. At its worst, it has spawned those vacuous horrors where a lesson displays page after page of text, pausing every now and then to accept a single letter. (And sometimes claiming that calling the student by name proves it is individualized learning.) Again, scripted courseware at best is suited to some limited objectives, but for most complex learning, it is simply inadequate.

THE NEED FOR A METALANGUAGE: LEARNING ABOUT LEARNING

Imagine the difficulties in trying to learn a subject without being able to reflect on how you might approach it, what you know about it already, or where you need to concentrate more. When we learn English history, for example, we talk to ourselves not only about "Henry VIII" and "the English Reformation" (dates, places, facts) but about how to relate this information to other issues. Yet this is often impossible to do in courseware.

Student- and author-controlled courseware lack a "metalanguage," that is, a way for the student to talk about strategies, plans, and tactics— the things that we introspect about as we learn. Yet it's this very strategy of strategies that teachers try to encourage. Among the questions we might ask our students are these:

> Is this problem like others you've seen?
> What do you already know?
> What do you need to know?
> What's worked for you so far?

No one would suggest that the kind of sophistication allowing real responses to these questions will be easily built into courseware; but we shouldn't conclude that the absence of that quality and level of interaction is therefore inevitable. We need to reexamine, as a start, our design assumptions.

LEARNING: A COOPERATIVE VENTURE

Turning over control either to the student or to the author ignores the fact that learning is an active and finally cooperative act between two intelligences. The teacher may know the subject but the student knows the student. The trick is getting each to tell the other what he knows. That kind of exchange requires a middle ground of courseware design where key issues get aired: How and when should a lesson intervene? How much control should the student have over instructional decisions? That middle ground is the territory we'll next explore.

PROGRAMS THAT SHARE CONTROL

Saying that learning is a cooperative activity between two intelligences does not, of course, specify what shape that cooperation should take. There is, however, a growing body of research, mostly having strong artificial-intelligence roots, that addresses this. Such lessons are generally research projects and not available commercially. Yet they have much to say to us as we prepare to develop courseware on increasingly powerful machines. These programs, known as "Intelligent Computer-Assisted Instruction" (ICAI), variously define the teaching role as tutor, coach, participant in a conversation, or (as we've already discussed) master performer. O'Shea and Self (1983) have surveyed much of this work and have formulated a number of questions that designers of intelligent CAL have to think about:

> What makes a good question?
>
> Should a lesson act as an "articulate expert" and explain how *it* reaches its answer, step by step?
>
> When should a lesson simply give the right answer?
>
> Should a lesson follow students and comment only when they do something unusual or should it intervene more often?
>
> How and when should a lesson generate new examples for a student to work on?
>
> How should a lesson keep track of it own teaching ability with an eye to improving its strategies?

This is a formidable list. What it implies is the need for rules, designed into the lesson, that explicitly say, "IF some circumstance exists, THEN take these steps." Let's start by looking at a number of programs that have various such tutoring rules built in.

Socratic Strategies: The Lesson as Questioner

SCHOLAR (Carbonell 1970) was an effort to teach South American geography by means of a "mixed-initiative" program in which either student or program could ask questions of the other. Its basic strategy was "Socratic," presenting material designed to impel students to see their mistakes and misconceptions. However, its tutoring strategy was essentially limited to following up one question with another when the student erred.

WHY (Stevens and Collins 1977) extended SCHOLAR beyond teaching facts to teaching causality. Its basic strategy remained Socratic, assuming that by learning about specific cases first, students could then generalize to others. A student who knows about rainfall in the Amazon, for example, should be able apply that knowledge to rainfall in other places, like California.

WHY uses a set of heuristic strategies that formalize intervention. For example, if a student gives unnecessary factors in an explanation, then the lesson selects a counterexample to show why those factors don't hold. So, should the student suggest that rice needs lots of rainfall, the program counters with Egypt, which has little rainfall but still grows rice. In this way, WHY tries to get the student to see what's either necessary or irrelevant and then generalize from the specific case at hand.

What is important from a design perspective is that WHY—as do all the intelligent programs we discuss in the chapter—formalizes teaching strategies as a set of rules that can tell the lesson what to do in various circumstances. WHY's global tutoring strategy has two objectives:

1. improving the student's understanding of the causes of rain, starting with the most important factors and incorporating other, less obvious ones
2. improving the student's ability to apply these factors to new examples

This two-part strategy is further refined into rules that try to recognize and respond to specific types of student misconceptions. For example:

If the student makes an error of fact, the tutor corrects it.

If the student makes an error about something outside the current topic, the tutor does not give a detailed correction.

If the student overgeneralizes, the tutor gives counterexamples.

If the student offers irrelevant factors, the tutor gives counterexamples.

If the student tries to reach a conclusion too quickly, the tutor teaches reasoning skills.

Whatever the effectiveness of a particular strategy (not making detailed corrections, giving counterexamples), the design point to emphasize is that the different rules are an integral part of the courseware, just as is the representation of the domain or the student model. Because these strategies can be written as production rules (like the ones we saw in the chapter on master performers), they are straightforward to work with on computers.

Again, one need make no claim about the final effectiveness of any particular rule. However, designing lessons in this way means that a teaching strategy is no longer just somehow there, implicit or covert. By explicitly spelling out a tutoring rule, the designer consciously integrates it into the whole system of subject matter, student, and machine. And that is crucial in terms of a rational approach to design, implementation, evaluation.

A Reactive Learning Environment

SOPHIE (Brown, Burton, and de Kleer, 1982) also has rules, although it is less a tutorial than a learning environment, reacting to student's questions and solutions about troubles in electronic circuits. Its overall goal is to create a place where students can explore ideas on their own. As they make hypotheses about faults in electronic circuits, SOPHIE gives feedback about the logical validity of their solutions. SOPHIE can also generate counterexamples to show where the student's logic fails. The program combines both knowledge about a particular area (electronic trouble-shooting) and a limited natural-language interpreter to answer questions.

SOPHIE's strategy is to react to the student rather than, like SCHOLAR or WHY, sometimes assume the initiative in the exchange. However, the rules for intervening are still explicit. For example:

> If a student might want to know something about the voltage or current in the faulty circuit and how a circuit in good working order would compare, SOPHIE not only answers these questions but makes comments about their usefulness.

> If the student can make a hypothesis about what's wrong in the circuit, the program then evaluates the hypothesis to see if it's consistent with the data seen so far.

> If the student gives the right answer for what seems the wrong reason, then SOPHIE flags the answer as suspect, noting that the data doesn't support the solutions.

> If students offer solutions, SOPHIE notes which information available to them supports their hypotheses and which doesn't.

> If the student's hypothesis is wrong or inconsistent, SOPHIE explains why.[4]

SOPHIE's tutorial strategy theoretically can be used with any subject where the program can simulate the context the student works in. Using the knowledge derived from its simulation, such a program can respond to the student's requests for information. The question of what to choose next is answered partly by students who have their own ideas about what may be wrong. Those ideas are used to profile students, which in turn guides SOPHIE's intervention. The result is a very reasonable middle ground between student and author control.

---

[4] To do this requires sophisticated programming, to say the least. SOPHIE first simulates a circuit given to the student who then asks a question about it. SOPHIE interprets that question with a "semantic parser" and answers. Roughly the same technique is used for hypothesis testing and evaluation. The program examines the student's hypothesis about possible faults in the circuit, looking for logical consistency with the information available. It simulates the student's hypothesis about what is faulty in the circuit. If these values are different than SOPHIE's, the discrepancies become the cue to begin an explanation. SOPHIE can also generate hypotheses about what's wrong and then give them to students who are out of ideas.

The Lesson as Coach

Wumpus WUMPUS (Goldstein 1982) coaches players to play a game where they have to hunt the Wumpus (a dangerous beast). The "coach" (read "courseware") is an expert itself which can see how good a student's move is and how it could be better. Models of the student's skills are built up, with increasing and decreasing estimates of how capable students are. The coach uses this model to guide interactions with each player. In general, the strategy is to discuss the skills players have yet to show in their moves where those skills would produce better results. The strategies, as with WHY, are made explicit as a set of rules. For example:

> If a player could be overwhelmed with advice, simplify or reduce a complex principle to a simpler assertion.
>
> If there's evidence that the student already knows an explanation of a strategy, delete another explanation of it altogether, thereby cutting out the redundancies that cause boredom. If the coach has explained something one way, try another way the next time.
>
> The coach's rhetoric should vary the way explanations are given, sometimes making them extremely concrete and sometimes extremely general.

The program does far more complex things than are outlined here (especially when it comes to student modeling), but again the important thing for the moment is the way teaching strategies can be codified.

West Another program that adopts the computer-as-coach strategy is WEST (Burton and Brown, 1982). WEST teaches an arithmetic game whose object is to take three numbers, combine them with the usual arithmetic operators (+ / * −) so as to produce a result that becomes the number of squares a player can move on the WEST board. The complicating feature is that there are times when the biggest number isn't best; some squares let players leap ahead, others slow them down. Good WEST players try to calculate answers to reach the best squares. The WEST coach looks over the player's shoulder during the game, making suggestions and criticisms. The major problem for its teaching strategy is to know when to intervene so that the program offers helpful advice without interrupting too often. WEST's general solution is to let the players discover good moves with only discreet guidance from the program.[5]

---

[5] WEST's design assumes that learners actively construct understanding based on their prior knowledge of a task. This means that players have to be aware of the errors that cause wrong answers. Unlike the strict behavioral approach in which a wrong answer is discouraged (like much programmed instruction, for instance), WEST assumes that errors are useful in helping students construct their understanding. The tutor's job is to give the extra information so that students themselves can spot their problems and turn nonconstructive bugs into constructive ones. Too little help and learning will be inefficient; too much help and students won't learn to spot bugs on their own (and won't have much fun either).

When to interrupt and what to say depends—as with intelligent courseware generally—on both a student model and a built-in expert. In general, intervention takes place only when the expert would use a skill to make an especially good move that the player missed. Here are some examples of WEST's tutoring rules:

> If a player makes an error that can be explained two competing ways, repeat the strategy most recently discussed.

> If there is no proof that a particular concept has been learned, then stay with it.

> If an issue (that is, a concept) hasn't been aired recently, talk about it.

> If (and only if) the expert's move is genuinely better than the player's, intervene.

> If a player makes a good move, note and praise it.

> If a player who should know better makes a bad move, don't dwell on it.

> If a comment is called for but one has just been made, don't make a second consecutive one—the enjoyment of the game itself could suffer.

> If a specific weakness is found, give examples of the possible moves at that moment and say why one is clearly better.

TUTORING STRATEGIES THAT BUILD ON EXISTING PRODUCTION RULES

We require a master performer, of course, before we can have a set of rules to say when a lesson should intervene. If we can't develop a master performer on our own, we can sometimes build on someone else's. GUIDON (Clancy 1982), another program with very explicit rules about when to intervene, shows this. Designed to teach diagnostic problem solving to medical students, the program uses the expertise of MYCIN, a program that itself uses a set of production rules to choose the most appropriate antibiotic for a given infection. Both student and program can initiate dialogues that are tracked over extended periods of time, rather than just covering the most recent questions or decisions.

GUIDON uses some 200 tutoring rules, quite separate from expert knowledge about infection, to guide the dialogue. The rules say when and how to present diagnostic principles, build or modify the student model, and respond to the student. GUIDON's "T-rules" (that is, tutoring rules) are sensitive to the lesson's context: The program chooses which of them to call on as a function of how complex the material is, the student's understanding of it, and the goals for the current session.

We can best get a sense of GUIDON by looking at a few sample T-rules (somewhat reworded here for clarity):

IF the student says I-KNOW [referring to some fact],
AND MYCIN [the expert] says I-Don't-Know,
THEN ask the student for his explanation and evaluate it;
IF both know, invoke the procedure for discussing a completed topic.

This rule allows creative and innovative students (whose answers might be better than the expert's) to state their opinions and not be penalized for disagreeing. At the same time, it immediately marks a suspect area: If students are confident when the expert isn't, they're more likely wrong than brilliant. Here are some other rules:

IF there are expert rules for this goal that have succeeded but have
    not yet discussed,
AND only one rule for this goal has succeeded,
AND there is strong evidence that the student has used this rule,
THEN simply state the rule and its conclusion.

IF the student has a correct hypothesis for a problem,
BUT there's no proof he knows *why* it's correct,
THEN ask for the relevant factors to support hypothesis
AND ask why the alternative one is discredited.

Other general GUIDON strategies include providing orientation to new tasks, making transitions between topics, and giving encouragement to make use of the data already gathered. The program also probes students' understanding when it's not sure what they know, directly confirms or corrects them, and reminds them of what methods they already know. GUIDON is a large and complex program, and one can continue describing it at length. For our purposes, it shows the potential for designing tutorial rules based on existing expert systems.

INTELLIGENT SUPPORT SYSTEMS

So far, we've been using the metaphors of master/apprentice and coach/player to describe the relationship between courseware and student. Let's change the metaphor somewhat to an "intelligent assistant" whose task it is to provide support to someone learning. An intelligent assistant can help students clarify their ideas by drawing on its own expertise at key moments. As Pangaro and Nicoll (1983) put it, the role of an intelligent assistant is not to override the student but to "confront [him] with the nature of his own decisions." The assumption is that learners are not entirely helpless, although they may lack skills or knowledge and are liable to overlook important factors. An intelligent assistant monitors the student's progress, interjecting and offering its knowledge. Like a coach, it is an expert; unlike a coach, it does not insist on its expertise.

The intelligent assistant metaphor shifts the students' role too. Rather than students being simply passive consumers of education, the metaphor suggests that they take an active role in their own learning and contribute more to the exchange than merely right or wrong answers. We can think of machine and student conversing; and, indeed, an important theoretical starting point is the Conversation Theory of Gordon Pask (1976; 1975).

CONVERSATION THEORY

Conversation Theory begins with the assumption that learning results from the structured conversations between two participants—the traditional teacher and student, courseware and student, or even two parts of the same intelligence (as when we converse with ourselves). The goal of a conversation is to reach an "understanding" or "agreement" between participants who talk about a mutually agreed-upon subject in a mutually agreed-upon language. Agreements are reached only when the student demonstrates a set of procedures such that an external observer (which can be a computer program) would say that they match the teacher's, human or otherwise.

A conversation in this sense, therefore, forces participants to "exteriorize" their cognitive activity, making their concepts public and open to inspection. The designer's role, however, goes beyond merely presenting information and monitoring the student. It begins with the creation of an "entailment structure," or map of the knowledge the lesson will teach.[6] Figure 11.1 shows a greatly abbreviated entailment mesh.

A topic can't exist without relation to others; it must be part of a network of interconnections showing mutual support. The structure of such a network must be coherent, consistent, and cyclic, so that any single topic can be derived from the others. The arrangement of topics in an entailment network is structured but not ordered into a hierarchy where one single topic is most important. (In a "pruning" process, one topic can be chosen temporarily as a kind of head or topic node of the network, but that depends on what the teaching calls for at that moment, not anything intrinsic in the material itself.) Such an entailment structure forms the

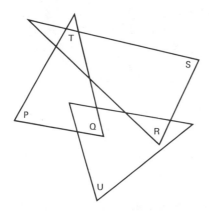

Figure 11.1   An Entailment Mesh

[6] Pask and his associates have developed THOUGHTSTICKER and CASTE which help the expert both articulate his knowledge and assemble the teaching materials.

rough equivalent of the master performer we've discussed, although the network representation requires quite different programming than production rules.

From a systems perspective, the entailment network theoretically permits the system enough starting points to match the variety and individuality of the student who will go through it and who masters topics along the way. The paths students take are not scripted in advance but are the results of a cooperative choosing between the students and courseware.

CASTE: AN IMPLEMENTATION OF CONVERSATION THEORY

An implementation of some of Conversation Theory is CASTE (for Course Assembly System and Tutorial Environment), which allows an expert to build an entailment mesh and the student to interrogate it. CASTE begins by having a subject-matter expert articulate the key topics in a subject and their interrelationships. It notes conflicts and inconsistencies as entailment meshes are built or added to and prompts the author to seek a resolution of any such conflict. CASTE thus forces experts to clarify their own thoughts so that similarities and distinctions in the domain are clear. Indeed, CASTE grew out of THOUGHTSTICKER, which Pask (1976) describes as an "epistemological laboratory."

In a CASTE lesson, students do not create or add to a mesh but explore it. They begin by choosing, for instance, a topic from the available ones, and CASTE searches out all "coherences" (that is, sets of relationships) around that topic and presents them to students who learn what they *don't* know in terms of what they *do* know. For example:

> IF the student wants to learn Topic A
> AND Topic A can be derived from Topic B and Topic C
> AND the student knows Topic B
> THEN present Topic C
> AND present Topic A in terms of Topic B and Topic C

Teaching Topic C requires that the student learn, or already know, other topics. The program assumes an entry level in which certain topics are primitives and do not themselves need explanation.

As more things are learned, the system helps students choose new topics by presenting those that are related to the greatest number of previously learned ones. For example:

> IF the student selects a topic to study
> THEN choose the explanation of that topic which has the greatest
>   number of previously understood topics

In "strict" CASTE, students must manipulate a model of the subject matter to demonstrate that they've grasped a concept. In "loose" CASTE, students can simply assert that they understand; this simplifies programming although it adds some uncertainty. When the system believes the student does understand a topic, it marks that topic as learned. It can then use this topic should it be part of another coherence that connects to a further new topic and which the student also wants to learn.

Students, then, move through the network, picking topics with the advice of the program. They can go to any one they wish, just as they could with a live tutor, including returning to something previously looked at. The program records whether they have seen something before and accordingly gives a new demonstration of it. As students learn more about a subject, the courseware learns more about them, particularly about what constitutes the "shared vocabulary." That knowledge is used by the system to make its instructional decision.

Pangaro (1983) likens such a decision to "deciding in conversation whether to use words which have already been established as shared, or to risk an explanation that contains words which may not be known or shared." The same knowledge can structure the presentation of topics if the student wants more direction. In that case, the program can make most of the choices. But whether it's the student or courseware that directs the path, the chances of learning are increased. The basic strategy is to use the maximum number of topics already marked as known to present new material.

In a CASTE lesson, unlike most courseware, it's not the designer alone who chooses what is simple and complex for the student or what wrong answers are most likely. The designer does determine relationship among the concepts being taught but not the order of their presentation. Students, therefore, can direct the sequence of instruction, subject to the system's advice about what they must know to proceed. This allows CASTE, for example, to present some concepts before others are fully understood. Far more than scripted courseware, the system is like a live tutor who allows students at least to explore ideas without having to master others first.[7]

COMCON: A CONVERSATIONAL SUPPORT SYSTEM

An example of courseware that uses some of the same ideas as CASTE is COMCON (for COMMA CONVERSER), an intelligent support and tutor-

---

[7] CASTE also insists on a demonstration of the behavior of a system in dynamic and often pictorial terms. It allows the student to manipulate inputs of a model and see the behavior of a system under various conditions. An example of this might be a steam engine simulation, which permits the student to vary heat and valve settings. A graphic display responds with increased temperature readings, faster motions, and perhaps explosions. This contrasts with other courseware where there's seldom a way to demonstrate the behavior of a system—unless the author has a great deal of programming sophistication. CASTE can then measure what's been learned far better than the multiple-choice, fill-in-the-blank question. In CASTE, the student demonstrates understanding by manipulating a model: this means that not just rote playback but something novel, not seen before, is brought out of the student. In the TEACHBACK mode, what is taught back is the dynamic relationships among topics. To continue with the above example: the student must increase the speed of the steam engine without increasing its heat (he opens a valve and the system sees if the speed increases). Manipulating the model shows his understanding; it exteriorizes the agreement between student and program.

ing system that teaches high school and college-level students about punc-tuation—specifically, the comma (Keller 1982). Unlike other grammar lessons that depend on prepared or "canned" sentences, COMCON allows students to enter any sentence they wish. The courseware then begins a conversation with the student about the correctness of the sentence's punctuation. This necessitates COMCON first having a master performer's knowledge of a properly punctuated sentence. That model enables COMCON to form an internal representation of the student's sentence, a model that is updated as the conversation goes forward.

The obvious advantage of such a program is that it responds to the student's needs. Rather than trying to estimate what kind of sentence to pick from a bank of already written ones, the courseware uses student sentences, which it assumes reflect present abilities. A single sentence, of course, will not show the student's full range of skills; but several are likely to be enough, especially when drawn from their own essays.

COMCON'S BASIC STRATEGY: A COOPERATIVE CONVERSATION

COMCON's basic strategy is to take a sample of student work and initiate a conversation about the things that make up the sentence (main clauses, introductory elements, conjunctions, and so on). Once these elements have been recognized (which is often the hardest part for student to master), the courseware has the student follow the relatively simple rules about how they should be punctuated. As the conversation goes on, students are prompted to introspect about what they've written, to externalize and compare it to the punctuation model used by COMCON's master per-former.

COMCON must form an internal representation of the sentence it has invited the student to enter, and to do that, it looks for key features. For example, it searches for coordinating conjunctions since these often mark the start of new main clauses. Similarly, it looks for subordinate conjunc-tions and prepositions (especially at the start of main clauses) and conjunc-tive adverbs. All these indicate the features of sentences (main or dependent clauses, nonessential elements, etc.) that students need to know if they are to punctuate their sentences correctly.

ASKING STUDENTS FOR HELP

COMCON's internal representation of the sentence doesn't mean that COMCON has a built-in natural-language processor that can understand whatever the student writes. COMCON merely has a list of features to look for and flag for discussion. For example, its tutoring strategy includes these rules:

> IF the sentence contains a coordinate conjunction (*and* or *but* or *or* . . .)
> THEN ask the student if it joins two main clauses

IF the student says the coordinate conjunction does not join two
main clauses,

THEN ask if it joins two coordinate elements

IF the student says the coordinate conjunction does not join two
coordinate elements,

THEN ask if it joins the last element in a series

Knowing about the presence of these features cues COMCON to begin a
conversation. However, it cannot tell by itself, for instance, whether or not
a group of words constitutes a complete thought. For that, it depends upon
the student.

It might seem paradoxical to call on a student who, after all, by
definition does not know the subject. But although students may not always
know rules of punctuation, they are almost sure to know if things make
sense. *When worlds collide* seems grammatical, but most students will
recognize that by itself, it's not a complete thought.

USING THE STUDENT AS A SEMANTIC PROCESSOR

COMCON requires, then, students to be the semantic processor it lacks.
Students and COMCON work together: The program uses its knowledge of
rules and its power to flag significant features; students use their ability to
see meaning or its absence. COMCON is not all-knowing in its pronouncements but instead reminds students of what they should know, directing
their attention to what they may have overlooked. It is the student who has
the final say and can override the program's advice.

WHAT-ABOUT QUESTIONS: COMCON CAN DIRECT THE
STUDENT'S ATTENTION

If the student has missed something that COMCON thinks may be important, it asks a "What-About" question and directs the student's attention to
what might have been overlooked. For instance, suppose the student wrote
this:

"When he was ready the man threw the ball and the boy caught it."

COMCON's questions would begin with

"Is there a coordinate conjunction?"

There is in this case (*and*), and if the student fails to see that, the program
offers a reminder:

"What about *and*?"

It then goes on to ask:

"Does the coordinate conjunction *and* join two main clauses?"

Since *and* does, it should have a comma in front of it. However, if the student doesn't know if there are two main clauses in the sentence, the program can isolate groups of words and have the student think about them:

"What about *The boy caught it*? Can it stand by itself and make sense?"

And so on through the various constituent parts of the sentence.

GETTING AND USING THE INFORMATION COMCON NEEDS

Although the program asks two "What-About" questions in the example above (about *and* and the things it joins), it can answer only the first by matching the word *and* against its list of coordinate conjunctions. That's all it is certain about. The second question requires semantic processing to know that *The boy caught it* is a complete thought and a main clause. The program needs the student to tell it that. But once it has that knowledge, it can turn to the student and say

"You have two main clauses joined by the coordinate conjunction *and;* you need a comma in front of it like this: *When he was ready the man threw the ball, and the boy caught it.*"

Similarly, COMCON can isolate the first main clause, noting that it begins with a subordinate conjunction but lacks any comma in the clause. Its "What-About" question will be

"What about *when*? Does *when* starts an introductory subordinate clause?"

It will then prompt the student to mark the end of the clause (*ready*); that done, COMCON shifts the clause to the end (The man threw the ball *when he was ready*) and asks if the sentence still makes the same sense. If the student replies that it does, COMCON will then say

"You have an introductory clause beginning with *when* and ending in *ready;* you need a comma after it like this: When he was ready, the man threw the ball."

And so with other features. In all cases, the strategy depends on reciprocity between two intelligences. The program exploits what the computer and student each do best until ultimately COMCON can generate a new and corrected version of the original sentence.

DEVELOPING GENERAL STRATEGIES

COMCON's primary object is not to produce correct sentences. Rather, the conversations are to develop the student's general strategies for correcting errors on all sentences, not just the ones he's just written. Field tests have shown that it prompts students to look for key features, internalizing the punctuation algorithm of COMCON's master performer (Keller 1982). In its most general form, that algorithm says, "Look for the presence or absence of a feature and select a rule to punctuate it." In time, the student will have both the computer's power to recognize patterns and the human power to put them into context. COMCON's conversations, therefore, constitute a "metalanguage," a way of talking about what one is doing in approaching the problem of punctuation. This metalanguage does not concern itself with one particular sentence (as we'd have with a canned sentence) but with sentences generally.

COURSEWARE, NOT A MAGIC MACHINE

Of course, if the object were to produce a sentence correcter—a magic machine, as it were—the "What-About" strategy wouldn't work. But in teaching, we want students to know more than just the right answer. We want them to know the process by which that answer was reached. In getting students to consider or reconsider an object and their treatment of it, COMCON tries to be like a human tutor. It doesn't say "right" or "wrong" (at least immediately) but directs the learner to look at something. Moreover, the student's answer to the "What-About" questions causes COMCON to modify its model of the sentence. The exchanges sharpen, therefore, both the student and COMCON. In reducing COMCON's uncertainty about what it sees (a main clause? a nonessential element?), students enable the program to assist them in learning the master performer algorithm.[8]

COMCON was written with fairly limited computing facilities. Even so, it demonstrates the feasibility of teaching language skills by going beyond the simple frame and canned sentence. Its master-performer and modeling facilities make possible limited conversations with students about their sentences, thereby responding to variety in the individual rather than attenuating it. COMCON makes some mistakes, of course, depending as it does on students to act as its semantic processor. But that dependence becomes an advantage: Learning proceeds as a conversation about sentences in general instead of a set of pronouncements about the correctness of a single sentence.

---

[8] COMCON encompasses more than is outlined here. The program also includes student-modeling facilities, which track the student's progress over many sentences. (We saw a brief example of how that information would work in the chapter on student modeling.) As COMCON sees problems develop or be resolved, it alters its global advice. It also contains an online HELP facility that students access when they forget a rule or the meaning of a term. Extensions to the program could call for asking the student *why* he made a mistake (forgotten rules, not being able to recognize elements, etc.) and instituting appropriate remediation. But the basic teaching metaphor remains the same: an intelligent tutor, responding to the student's sentence, directing him to introspect about what he's done.

SUMMARY

We have looked at a number of tutoring strategies and metaphors for courseware that tell a lesson when to intervene. We began with two that are at opposite ends of the courseware continuum:

> *Student control* permits students to choose whatever topics they wish when they wish. Its weakness is that it does not give the student sufficient direction.

> *Author control* of instructional decisions generally is the norm in scripted courseware. Its weakness as a tutoring strategy is that it does not sufficiently take into account individual patterns and the variety of learners.

We then considered intelligent courseware, which occupies the middle ground, as it were, both intervening and offering students a role in choosing what learning takes place. Examples are

> *Socratic:* a questioning tutor controls a dialogue that attempts to impel students to see their mistakes.

> *Reactive learning environment:* the lesson reacts to student questions and hypotheses by simulating the effects of student ideas and presenting the implications.

> *Computer coach:* the lesson looks over the shoulder of students, offering advice at appropriate moments.

> *Intelligent assistant:* the lesson acts as a participant in a conversation with the student, seeking to reach understandings with the student about concepts in a particular domain.

These intelligent strategies are rule-based; that is, the courseware design includes explicit rules for taking instructional decisions. All face at least three major problems:

1. Courseware cannot directly find out from the student what it needs to know, and so instructional decisions must be based on partial and inferential knowledge.
2. Courseware lacks a practical natural-language interface; this makes communicating with the student difficult.
3. There is no general theory of instruction that would tell courseware what to do at any given moment.

REFERENCES

Brown, J. S., Burton, R. R., and de Kleer, J. "Pedagogical, Natural Language and Knowledge Engineering Techniques in SOPHIE I, II, and III," in Sleeman, D. and Brown, J. S. *Intelligent Tutoring Systems* (London: Academic Press, 1982), pp. 227–282.

Burton, R. R. and Brown, J. S. "An Investigation of Computer Coaching for Informal Learning Activities," in Sleeman, D. and Brown, J. S. *Intelligent Tutoring Systems* (London: Academic Press, 1982), pp. 79–98.

Carbonell, J. "AI in CAI: An Artificial Intelligence Approach to Computer-Assisted Instruction," *IEEE Transactions on Man-Machine Systems,* MMS–11 (4) (December 1970), pp. 190–202.

Clancy, W. J. "Tutoring Rules for Guiding a Case Method Dialogue," in Sleeman, D. and Brown, J. S. *Intelligent Tutoring Systems* (London: Academic Press, 1982) pp. 201–226.

Gagne, R. M, Wager, W. and Rojas, A. "Planning and Authoring Computer-Assisted Lesson Instructions," *Educational Technology,* 5 (September 1981), pp. 17–26.

Goldstein, I. P. "The Genetic Graph: A Representation for the Evolution of Procedural Knowledge," in Sleeman, D. and Brown, J. S. *Intelligent Tutoring Systems* (London: Academic Press, 1982), pp. 51–78.

Keller, A. *The Comma Converser* (unpublished Ph.D. dissertation, Concordia University, Montreal, Canada, 1982).

Merrill, M. D., Schneider, E. W., and Fletcher, K. A. TICCIT (Englewood Cliffs, N.J.: Educational Technology Publications, 1980).

O'Shea, T. and Self, J. *Learning and Teaching With Computers* (Englewood Cliffs, N.J.: Prentice-Hall, 1983).

Pangaro, P. *CASTE: Course Assembly System and Tutorial Environment* (Washington, D.C.: PANGARO, 1983).

Pangaro, P. and Nicoll, J. F. *Deleting the Knowledge Engineer* (Washington, D.C.: PANGARO, 1983).

Papert, S. *Mindstorms* (New York: Basic Books, 1980).

Pask, G. *Conversation, Cognition, and Learning* (Amsterdam and New York: Elsevier, 1975).

Pask, G. *Conversation Theory: Applications in Education and Epistemology* (Amsterdam and New York: Elsevier, 1976).

Stevens A. and Collins A. "The Goal Structure of a Socratic Tutor," in *Proceedings of the Association for Computing Machinery Annual Conference,* 1977.

Winograd, T. "Computer Software for Working With Language," *Scientific American,* 251 (3) (September 1984), 130–45.

Index